CARING FOR INSECT LIVESTOCK:
An Insect Rearing Manual

Compiled and edited by
Gary A. Dunn, M.S., F.R.E.S.
Director of Education
Young Entomologists' Society, Inc.
1915 Peggy Place
Lansing MI 48910-2553

Portions of this manual were previously published in T.I.E.G. Magazine (published by the Teen International Entomology Group), Y.E.S. Quarterly and Insect World (published by the Young Entomologists' Society, Inc.) and Michigan 4-H Manual #1406 (written by Gary A. Dunn and published by the Michigan State University Cooperative Extension Service).

ACKNOWLEDGEMENTS
The following people have provided information or contributed to this manual: John Acorn, Peter Aindow, David J. Albaugh, Susan Andres, George W. Beccaloni, Rose Mary Blanchard, Rick Bochelt, Jo Brewer, Paul D. Brock, Milan Busching, James J. Carthy, Chris Conlan, Karen D. Creamer, Guido Dingerkus, David Eppelheimer, Brain O.C. Gardiner, Jeffrey C. Gilbert, Thomas Greager, Roger Hoopingarner, Marion Mahler, Walter McKinney, W.W. McLaren, Lawrence J. Moore, Lawrence J. O'Connor, William D. O'Donnell, Ted Pike, Melvin Pritchard, Robin Renner, Lisa Resotko, Joe Robertson, R.I. Sailer, Richard J. Sauer, Richard J. Snider, Stephen M. Spomer, Karen Strickler, John J. Symborski, Jr., Roy Van Driesche, John A. Wilcox, and Barb Wittman.

Published by:
Young Entomologists' Society, Inc.
1915 Peggy Place
Lansing MI 48910-2553
(517) 887-0499

ISBN 1-884256-10-4

CONTENTS

INTRODUCTION

PART I: BASIC REARING TECHNIQUES

PART II: INSECT REARING

INTRODUCTION

WHY REAR INSECTS?

Many entomology projects emphasize the study and handling of dead specimens. Most people who set up their own insect collections are careful observers, as well as collectors. They know that the more they learn and understand about insect activity, the easier it will be for them to collect the insect specimens they prize. Observing and collecting insects are both extremely important parts of entomology. To fully understand insects, people must have firsthand knowledge of insect ways and means of living: how insects feed, grow, behave, disperse and reproduce. This knowledge can only be gained by studying live insects. Live insects can be observed and studied in their natural environment or in captivity. Observing insects in captivity is the most convenient method of studying live insects.

Many collectors rear insects to obtain perfect adult specimens of the uncommon and rare species, with minimal impact to natural populations. Other collectors are hoping to obtain representatives of the various immature stages, so that they can document the all-too-frequently ignored (or unknown) immature stages of many insect species.

In recent years there have been efforts to raise certain butterflies and moths on special "butterfly farms". Here, with lots of tender loving care by humans, a greater percentage of the larvae reach adulthood successfully. Some of these adults may be sold as preserved specimens (thereby protecting wild populations), but many will be released to help bolster native populations.

Reared Insects as Science Projects

Live insects can be the basis for many fascinating, low-cost (often free) science projects. Most insect species complete their life cycles in relatively brief spans. They take up little space, and their maintenance requirements are often fairly simple.

Rearing insects can provide valuable learning experiences. Observing insects as they grow and change from one stage to another is certainly interesting, but live insect studies help gather important scientific information on the duration of insect life stages (under varying conditions), insect mating behavior, feeding behavior, and response to environmental stimuli.

There are two approaches to conducting an insect rearing project: long-term or short-term rearing studies.

Long-term Projects. Select one or more insect species and try to rear them through several generations. Here are some items that should be part of your project. (1) Record notebook: Keep a journal of everything you did, the type of container or cage you used, the type and amount of food you fed the insects, and the rearing conditions (temperature, humidity, light, etc.) (2) Reproduction rate: Count or estimate the number of individuals in your culture at regular intervals (weekly or monthly). (3) Problems: Describe any problems you encountered, whether solved or unsolved! Report the problems you ran into (like insect diseases, parasites, starvation or accidents) and tell how you handled these situations. (4) Life cycle: Collect and preserve representative specimens from each life stage to show the complete life cycle of the insect species you studied. Keep notes on the life cycle of your insects and how long it takes them to complete their development at certain temperatures. (5) Educational displays: Prepare a notebook, picture album, display or slide program so you can share with others what you learned from your project.

Short-term Projects. Even if you are only able to observe insect cultures (either your own or someone else's) for a short period of time, you can still conduct a study project. Here are some of the items you may want to observe and report on: (1) Life stages: Which are present? Which are absent? How much time is spent in each stage? How active are the various stages? (2) Requirements for life: What are they, and what evidence do you see to support your conclusions? (3) Reproduction: How do the insects mate and reproduce?

In all cases, when you are done with your project, return the insects to the place where you found them (or their native habitat).

Making Money with Live Insects

Did you know that you can make money raising and selling some insects? Well it's true! Here are some examples.

Beekeeping. You may already be familiar with the potential of honey bees as a source of income. In addition to selling honey and beeswax, many beekeepers also rent their hives to farmers who need bees to pollinate their crops. Hive rentals become more important every day because soon there may not be enough wild bee colonies in any given area to pollinate all the crops that need it. Beekeeping can be quite involved, and so you will probably need the guidance of an experienced beekeeper. Your county Cooperative Extension Service office can help you find brochures and publications on beekeeping, as well as knowledgable resource people, so this topic is not covered in this manual.

Fish Bait. Many insects are used as bait by anglers. The popularity of any bait insect depends on the area where you live; therefore, you will need to determine which insects are in demand in your area. Popular fish bait insects include crickets, wax moth larvae (waxworms) and mealworms.

Pet Food. Many people keep lizards and tarantulas as pets, and insects are the primary food source for these animals. Many of the insects that can be used for fish bait, especially crickets and mealworms, can also be used to feed exotic pets.

Biological Supply Companies. Some biological supply companies buy selected insects in large quantities for resale to schools and research institutions. The specimens are then used for teaching or biological research. The insect needs of these companies are constantly changing, so contact them for an up-to-date list of the insect species they need and for shipping instructions. The names and addresses of companies that buy insect specimens can be found in "The Insect Study Sourcebook" by Gary A. Dunn (see bibliography).

Selling Livestock to Other Rearers. Many insect rearers support their rearing operation by selling off surplus livestock to other rearers. This benefits both the seller and the buyer of insect livestock. Of course, many rearers also prefer to trade livestock, rather than purchase it.

Selling Livestock to Butterfly Houses and Insect Zoos. In recent years butterfly houses and insect zoos have become very popular, and many exhibits are now in operation in the United States and Canada (as well as overseas). Although some of these facilities often raise their own livestock for display, they are always looking for livestock suppliers with new and different livestock to offer. Those facilities that do not have in-house rearing facilities, and that buy and release their livestock, are certainly interested in learning about reliable suppliers of butterflies, moths and other exotic insects. The world's most comprehensive list of butterfly houses and insect zoos (complete with names and addresses) can be found in "The Insect Study Sourcebook" by Gary A. Dunn (see bibliography).

PART I: BASIC REARING TECHNIQUES

SELECTING AND OBTAINING LIVE INSECTS

There are some important questions you need to consider when deciding on what insect species to rear. For example, is the insect an appropriate size for the space you have? Is the insect harmless? Will it cause problems if it escapes? Are there interesting features about the appearance, behavior or life cycle of the species? Is the insect adaptable to culturing? Will it mate in captivity? Some of the questions mentioned above are answered in the rearing instructions in this manual. The others can only be answered through your own experimentation. You can start your live insect cultures two ways: purchase insects from biological supply companies or collect your own. The choice between buying or collecting is often influenced by how much money you have, the season you want to start your rearing, the species you decide on, and how much time you have to hunt for insects.

Collecting Your Own Insects to Rear

Obviously, gathering your own specimens costs virtually nothing, but more importantly, it helps you understand the habitat and natural conditions of the species you will be raising.

The equipment you will need to gather insects is not elaborate. For terrestrial and arboreal insects all you really need are your fingers and a collecting carton. However, you may also want to use a garden trowel, forceps, aspirator, insect traps or other tools depending on the insects you wish to collect. For aquatic insects you will need a dip net and a pail or similar container.

Terrestrial and arboreal insects collected in the field should be carried in a special collecting carton. Ordinary plastic, glass and metal containers are not satisfactory because they don't "breathe." This can cause your specimens to overheat, mold and die. The best collecting containers are made from quart-sized, cylindrical, unwaxed cardboard cartons (like an ice cream carton). Cartons should be available locally from paper manufacturers or from retail stores that handle ice cream, oysters, delicatessen items or other perishable goods. Cylindrical cartons are best, but those with tapered sides can also be used. Cut out the bottom of the carton and replace it with window screen or cheesecloth. Cut a 5/8-inch to 1-inch hole in the side of the carton about one-third of the way down from the screened end. The exact location of this hole is not critical. Block the hole with a cork. You'll probably want several collecting containers, since you may need one or more for storage at any given time.

When you use the collecting carton, hold it so that the screening is at the top and the removable lid is at the bottom. Put the insects in the carton through the circular hole in the side. Since insects tend to move "uphill," you will find that they congregate at the top of your carton. This means your insects won't try to escape every time you open the entryway. To reduce the insect activity in your collecting carton, cover it loosely with a dark cloth. When it's time to transfer the specimens to a rearing cage you may need to further reduce their activity to keep them from escaping or being hurt. You can do this by placing the insects (in their container) in the refrigerator (not the freezer) until their activity slows, then you can easily place them in a rearing cage.

Aquatic insects should be transported in a loosely covered container. Those insects that breathe through plastron respiration (for example water striders, water boatmen, backswimmers, and diving beetles) should be transported in a container filled with wet, crumpled paper towels. Do not transport them in water-filled containers. The wave action in the container will watersoak their oxygen-laden body hairs, making it difficult for them to breathe. If your aquatic insects do become waterlogged, simply dry them on paper towelling for a few minutes to restore the hairs' effectiveness. Those insects which breathe with gills (for example, dragonflies, damselflies, mayflies and stoneflies) should be transported directly in water (pond water or river water works best).

Obtaining Insect Livestock by Mail

Many species of insects not native to the United States are available for rearing by purchasing them from suppliers in other countries. By purchasing live insects through the mail you may be able to rear and study exotic insects that may be quite spectacular. Directions for rearing some of these exotic species are given in this manual. The names and addresses of many companies and individuals that sell live insect specimens can be found in "The Insect Study Sourcebook" by Gary A. Dunn (see bibliography). Some entomological publications, such as "Flea Market" and "Ecdysis", are dedicated to helping livestock buyers and sellers network with one another. Other entomological periodicals, such as "Blattodea Culture Group Newsletter", "Bulletin of the Amateur Entomologists Society", "Coleopterists Bulletin", "Entomological News", "Entomologische Zeitschrift Mit Insektenborse", "Newsletter of the Exotic Entomology Group", and "Sciences Nat", have small "bulletin board" sections with offers of livestock (see "The Insect Study Sourcebook" by Dunn).

Permits for Exotic Insect Livestock

The state and federal departments of agriculture have regulatory authority over the importation and interstate movement of non-native plant pests, pathogens and vectors. These regulations are necessary to protect American agriculture by preventing the entry of new pest organisms into the United States from foreign areas and to prevent their spread within the nation. These regulations are concerned with any movements into the United States or Territories, as well as between points within the U.S.A.

In past years it was only necessary to file for a permit when the insects in question were known plant pests. Currently it is strongly suggested to file the necessary paperwork under Category C (courtesy category) even for non-pest species, as this will prevent confiscation or delay of shipment for verification of status (in either case this would probably be fatal to your livestock).

If you intend to import or move exotic insect species you will need a permit from your state agricultural officials and the U.S. Department of Agriculture, Animal and Plant Health Inspection Service - Plant Protection and Quarantine (PPQ-APHIS). A PPQ Form 526 can be obtained from your state Department of Agriculture (usually Division of Plant Industry, or similar division). Forms and additional information may also be obtained from the Director, Programs Development and Application, PPQ-APHIS, U.S. Dept. of Agriculture, Federal Building, Hyattsville, MD 20782. Plant Protection and Quarantine field offices can also supply the information (check your local phone book for the office nearest you). This form should be filed with the state regulatory agency at least 30 days in advance of expected receipt of your livestock. The application must be filed by the intended receiver of the shipment because he/she will be ultimately responsible for complying with state and federal regulations, including any special safeguards. If your application is approved, the state agency forwards it to the USDA PPQ-APHIS in Hyattsville, Maryland for approval. Upon approval the federal officials will notify their field staff at the expected port of entry to be on the lookout for your package.

Some of the standard safeguards for exotic livestock include: (1) insects must be shipped in sturdy, escape-proof containers; (2) all packing materials and shipping containers shall be sterilized or destroyed immediately upon receiving insects; (3) without prior notice and at reasonable hours, authorized PPQ and State regulatory officials shall be allowed to inspect the conditions under which the organisms are kept; and (4) all necessary precautions must be taken to prevent escape of pests; in the event of an escape, state and federal officials should be notified immediately.

Methods for Mailing Insect Livestock

How many times has this happened to you? You are eagerly awaiting the arrival of some livestock you ordered or traded for. The package comes and, upon opening it, you are greeted by a nice assortment of bug guts! In an attempt to keep this from happening again, here are some helpful hints for mailing pupae, ovae, larvae and adults. The guidelines presented here apply to Lepidoptera, but should also work for other orders as well (perhaps with a little modification from time to time).

Pupae and Cocoons: The easiest way to mail these is to pack them in a container that is then packed inside a small box. You can use an empty racquetball can or margarine container packed inside a small box with plenty of wadded newspaper or styrofoam pellets. Make sure the cocoons or pupae are well packed inside the inner container. They should not be rattling around in there!

Cocoons can take a fair amount of abuse since there is already a natural cushion of silk around the pupa. Just pack these in an inner container nice and snug. You can take up any extra space with cotton, tissue, or toilet paper. Actually, some cocoons are so tough (Hyalophora spp.) that they can be packed snugly into a single strong box and mailed without any extra protection.

Naked pupae and chrysalids require extra care since these tend to be more fragile. Placing them between layers of cotton in the inner container is recommended. For those that are specially soft or valuable it is advisable to wrap them individually with tissue and then layer them in the cotton. This sounds like a lot of trouble, but it's worth it because your shipment is practically guaranteed to arrive undamaged when shipped in this manner. When you get right down to it, you just spent two months painstakingly rearing those larvae until they pupated. You are now just one step away from the final product so spend an extra ten minutes and pack them right!

Ovae: Only about 75% of ova shipments ever arrive in sound condition. The problems are so easy to rectify that it's laughable. There are two major culprits contributing to the demise of ova in the mail worldwide.

First, aquarium tubing does not make a good mailing container! Just pick this stuff up and give it a squeeze. Overcooked broccoli is tougher! Shipments packed in this stuff almost never arrive in sound condition. Even when they do arrive safely, they are wedged so tightly in the middle of the tube that it is hard to get them out without breaking them. The problem is that the tubing is so soft and pliable that it expands and contracts with all of the temperature changes that it is exposed to during transit. This causes the ovae to settle in tighter and tighter during shipment and eventually some of them get crushed, either by postal machines, or other natural causes.

The second most common problem encountered is hostplant material sent with the ovae. There is a very good reason for avoiding this. When you cut hostplant it no longer gives off oxygen. In fact, it does just the opposite. Cut leaves will raise the amount of carbon dioxide in the surrounding atmosphere (especially in an enclosed container). Very often, the amount of carbon dioxide will get high enough that it kills the ovae before they hatch. Eggs seem to be very sensitive to CO_2 gas. The larvae, on the other hand can handle it quite well, but not the eggs.

And now, a foolproof egg mailing method: microtubes (also known as Eppendorph tubes). (One source we've found for microtubes is Phenix Research Products, tollfree at 1-800-767-0665; just ask for a catalog). These microtubes are great! They have a flip top lid for easy access and they are tough enough to run the postal gauntlet unscathed. They are made of polyethylene, so they are light, see-through and reusable. The best size to order is the 500 microliter size. This size will hold about 30 ovae the size of C. regalis or over one hundred ovae of smaller species. If you need a slightly larger container, then get the 1.5 milliliter size. This size will hold about 100 ovae of something the size of C. regalis or E. imperialis. Just remember to make small punctures in the lid of the microtubes with an insect pin to allow for some ventilation. Also, take up any excess space inside the tube with a bit of cotton so the ovae don't roll around so much. Oh, one more thing, make sure to slap an extra 10 cents postage on the envelop in case an over-eager postal clerk decides to measure the width!

Larvae and Adults: This is a bit more risky and expensive. If you are going to mail live larvae or adults, it is highly recommended that you use an overnight service, or at least a two day service. You can go to the post office and get some of their express mail boxes or priority mail boxes.

Pack the larvae in a zip-lock bag with enough hostplant to last two or three days (don't overpack the food). Then put a piece of paper towel in to absorb any excess moisture and poke a few holes in the bag for ventilation. Try to arrange the hostplant in the bag so that it is keeping the bag at least somewhat inflated. You do not have to use bags, any lightweight container that is big enough will do. For example, larvae can arrived in fine condition when shipped in old plastic vitamin bottles. Just remember to include some form of ventilation and moisture absorption.

For adults, most of the same conditions apply that you would use for larvae. You don't want them to dry out, suffocate, or starve to death. Feed the adults just before you mail them (if they eat as adults). Then put the butterfly or moth in a glassine envelope and place it in a tough, protective container of some sort. This container can be a old cassette case or a margarine tub or whatever, use your imagination. Make sure you spritz a little water in there before you close everything up to keep the humidity high. Some people place a small piece of cotton moistened with sugar water in the corner of the glassine envelope where the butterfly can sip from it during transit (especially for longer trips).

Basic Notes: The most important thing you can do is use your common sense. For instance, don't send live larvae to your friends in North Dakota in the middle of January. The larvae will probably be popsicles by the time they reach the state line. If sending larvae or adults, give the person on the receiving end a call so they can make preparations. And finally, never assume that just because you wrote "fragile" all over your package that it is going to get special treatment!

BASIC CONSIDERATIONS AND REARING TECHNIQUES

It is very important to match the natural habitat of the insects you want to rear, including their preferred food and proper light, temperature and humidity conditions. You will need a cage or other container in which to rear most insects. The type of container you use will depend on the type and number of insects you decide to raise (see pages 8 to 15). But no matter what type of rearing container you select, it must be constantly tended. For example, insects won't eat dried leaves, and without a constant fresh food and a source of water the insects will quickly die.

Insects that feed on live plants can be caged over potted plants or fed fresh material from their host plants. With a little ingenuity, a suitable cage can be designed to accommodate your rearing plans. The important thing is to keep the cage tight enough to restrain the insects and still provide enough ventilation that the container doesn't "sweat" and the food material gets moldy. Loose, slightly moist soil and leaf litter should also be provided in case the insect likes to burrow or pupates in or on the ground (see page 15).

Terrestrial insects and scavengers do well in containers with a small amount of substrate in the bottom (see page 15). Keep the cage clean and control moisture to prevent molds and diseases.

You may also find it interesting to dig large larvae and pupae out of soil or rotten logs and rear them to the adult stage. The larvae probably won't need to be fed as long as you keep some of the rotten wood or soil in the container with the specimens. Place the larvae and soil or wood in a closed jar or other container to retain moisture, and check them periodically. You may be surprised to find freshly-emerged specimens of some of the largest and least common beetles and other insects. Remember that the life cycles of some of these large insects may be quite long, so you'll have to be patient. As long as the larvae are plump, moist and healthy-looking, they will probably complete development to adulthood. Unhealthy, diseased or dead individuals should be removed from the container and disposed of.

You can rear insects that infest plants (seeds, galls, leaves or stems) or other materials by placing the infested object in an enclosed container. Don't let such materials get too dry, or too moist (the materials and specimens could mold). If you want to easily gather specimens from such a culture, use an opaque container (one that you cannot see through) and insert an open-ended glass vial through a hole (just big enough for the lip of the vial) in one end of the container. As adult insects emerge from the infested material, they will be attracted to the light coming through the vial. Once they are in the vial, you can remove them for study or to add them to your personal insect collection.

Collecting moth cocoons and butterfly chrysalids is another interesting activity. You may get lucky and find a full-grown caterpillar that is just about to transform into a pupa. These can be collected and observed until the adult butterfly or moth emerges. Since some Lepidoptera overwinter as pupae you may have to wait until the following spring to see them emerge.

REARING CONTAINERS AND CAGES

Many kinds of containers and cages can be used to hold insects for rearing. You may use whatever type is available that suits the needs of your insects. A good insect rearing cage should be lightweight, sturdy, escapeproof and well-ventilated. It should also allow you to watch the insects easily.

Plastic Boxes

This method usually consists of a closed container of some sort that is made of plastic or a similar compound. Clear plastic boxes, such as freezer boxes, vegetable crispers or shoe boxes, are excellent. There should be a few vent holes in the top or a loose fitting lid to allow some fresh air in. Since the boxes are made of plastic, one can easily drill or heat-drill air holes in them. Many small holes may be drilled into the lid or you can make one or two larger air holes and cover them with screen, glued to the box. Use a glue suitable for plastic, and not a water-soluble one (like Elmer's) that will soften if a few drops of water gets on it. Insect and arachnid livestock with mandibles and pincers should be placed in containers with small holes and without screens. Large screened holes will not work well because these animals will patiently pry apart the screen with their mandibles or pincers until there is a hole large enough for escape. If, however, you will be keeping livestock that will have small young, the screen is much better than the drilled air holes at preventing the newborns from crawling through the small open holes. The bottom should have a layer of paper towels to absorb excess moisture. This should be changed periodically depending on the density and size of the larvae being reared. Raising the larvae and food a little off the bottom with a piece of 1/2 " hardware cloth is strongly advised. This permits the larvae to feed without coming into frequent contact with their frass.

They have numerous advantages that other cages don't offer. They are more or less unbreakable, so that even if dropped, they will not allow your livestock to escape. Probably the best thing about using plastic boxes is the small amount of space they use. They can be stacked and moved with ease. Most of them have grooved lids and bases so they fit together so they can be easily stacked; if you have a large number of animals, this can be a special advantage as the space they occupy can be minimized. This makes them convenient for people living in apartments or in other lack of space situations. The lids can be easily secured to the bases by placing a rubber band around the entire box, making it escape proof. They are easy to sterilize for reuse too; just soak them in bleach. Plastic boxes also allow you to use very small cuttings (or even just leaves) to feed your critters. This is nice if you are trying to minimize the pruning damage to your foodplants. Finally, you can use foodplants that do not hold up well when they are cut, like willow for instance.

Unfortunately, plastic boxes have many problems associated with them. By far, the worse problem is disease. Diseases can spread extremely fast in a plastic box. The reason is the stale, humid air environment that the box creates, combined with crowded conditions. Even in low densities in a plastic box the larval often come into contact with each other and their frass, thus spreading whatever contagious disease they may have. Also, as the larvae grow so does the frequency with which you must change the paper towels in the box. When larvae reach the late instars you may have to change the paper towels twice a day. This can become a royal pain after awhile. Plastic boxes also tend to get hotter than the surrounding temperature. This is OK if its cold in the house, but it only takes a few stray rays of sunshine to heat the box up to where it becomes a small oven. NEVER put a plastic box containing insect livestock in direct sunlight! You should not even bother trying to rear species that need arid conditions in a plastic box. The humidity, lack of moving air, and sunshine will probably kill them.

Plastic Bags

Rearing larvae in plastic bags has all the same ups and downs as rearing them in plastic boxes. Most of the same problems apply here with the only virtue being that the bags are disposable.

Screen Cylinders

This method consists of a piece of aluminum screen rolled to fit the inside diameter of a petri dish, jar lid, tuna can, cake pan, or similar container. You could even use two trash can lids and a hardware cloth cylinder over a bucket of water if you want a really big screen cylinder!
All you have to do is roll a piece of aluminum window screen so that it fits inside of the petri dish (or any other container). The screen cylinder should be about one foot high and just under five and one half inches in diameter. You can hold the cylinder to the proper diameter with staples or hot glue. Melt a hole in one of the petri dishes and place the bottom of the petri dish over a cup of water and slide the stems of the foodplant through the holes into the water. Block any unused holes with cotton or paper towel to prevent the insects from drowning. Then slide the screen cylinder over the foodplant until it rests firmly inside the lip of the petri dish. Place your insects on the foodplant and put the lid on top of the screen cylinder.

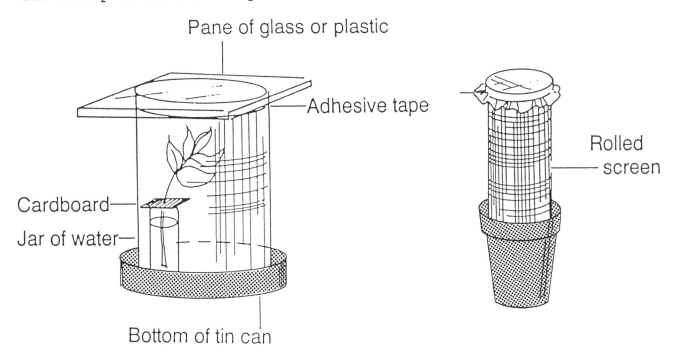

Pane of glass or plastic

Adhesive tape

Cardboard

Jar of water

Bottom of tin can

Rolled screen

This is a great way to raise caterpillars and other leaf feeding insects. The cylinders are easy to change and need less cleaning than a plastic box. They also give your insects a clean airy environment that is much less likely to breed disease. The cylinders don't take up much space and they are easy to move and sterilize. This allows you to put them in the window for some needed sunshine. Also, the insects are out where you can see them and watch them grow. This method has very few problems associated with it!

The only problems with using screen cylinders are minor ones. They can be a little unstable and easy to knock over sometimes. So all you clutz's out there be careful! You cannot use foodplants that do not hold up well after being cut. Also, it is difficult to rear large quantities of insects in one 5.5" cylinder, so you may want to design, construct and use larger screen cylinders.

You can make a very nice cylinder cage for insects not requiring live foodplants with some simple household materials. You will need 2 empty tuna fish or cat food cans (or any other shallow container like a spray can caps or cake pans), a bottle cap, a piece of screening (6" x 12", or 2" larger than circumference of cans), a twig, a half cup of plaster of

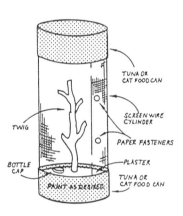

TUNA OR CAT FOOD CAN

SCREEN WIRE CYLINDER

TWIG

PAPER FASTENERS

BOTTLE CAP

PLASTER

TUNA OR CAT FOOD CAN

PAINT AS DESIRED

Paris, and a little water. Start by removing the labels and cleaning the cans. You can paint or decorate the outside of the cans if you like. Study the picture of the completed bug cage to familiarize yourself with how it's put together. Place the 1/2 cup of plaster of Paris into one of the cans (more of you're using a larger can!), and slowly add small amounts of water. Mix the plaster until it is smooth and pudding-like. Set your bottle cap (water dish) and twig into the plaster. Roll the screen into a tube and and push it down into the plaster next to the edge of the can. You may need to push some of the wet plaster up against the screen and the edge of the can. There should be at least an inch of overlap in the screen; you can staple, fasten, or glue the overlapped area together, if needed. Set the cage in a warm, dry place so the plaster can harden. Your second can is the lid. It slips down over the top of the cage, and can be removed to put insects in or to take them out.

For livestock requiring more humid conditions, use rolled acetate in place of the screening (and punch a few holes in the lid).

Rearing in Peat Pots

One of the greatest problems encountered in rearing insects, especially caterpillars, is disease. Many common rearing cages are reusable, but this carries with it the possibility of transmitting disease from one culture to another. Even with relatively sterile containers, the risk of disease is high, especially with rare specimens. In addition, some metals (like coffee cans) may be toxic to certain species.

Moisture is an important factor in insect rearing, as well. The moisture requirements for each species may vary, so the ideal container should allow good regulation of water. Jars and cans sometimes retain too much water, and unless proper safeguards are observed, disease could be more prevalent or the insect could even drown. Fungus grows rapidly in wet containers. By way of contrast, gauze and wire cages are often too dry, and the foodplants seldom last long. This makes for more work checking the containers and providing a food supply.

Lastly, while jars and cans are often easy to come by, specialized cages like cricket cages and glass compartments are often costly.

One seldom-mentioned container for rearing insects is the peat pot, a popular item for gardeners who start young plants indoors earlier than they can start them in the garden. Very simply, peat pots are containers of various sizes made from compressed peat or sphagnum moss. Sphagnum is entirely natural, absorbs water readily, and has other advantages over standard rearing cages.

Peat pots, unlike their glass and metal counterparts, have natural antiseptic properties. In fact, peat moss was used for bandages during World War I. And peat pots are easily treated to discourage disease. They can be heated in an oven to kill bacteria, or they can be dipped in boiling water. You can even spray the pot with commercial antiseptic, and  then rinse them to remove the alcohol. With this type of treatment, they can be used several more times with minimal disease risks. You can also use unmilled sphagnum moss for the bottom of the container to discourage fungus growth. One reason it limits disease spread is peat's ability to distribute water evenly over its surface. It dries quickly without vapor buildup, and insects can drink directly from the walls. If a moist environment is desired, simply stand the pot in moist sand. Otherwise, sprinkle daily with water.

In addition to these qualities, peat pots are inexpensive, especially if purchased in bulk quantities.

Peat pots are very easy to use and require only a covering of gauze, screen, cheesecloth or netting. You may want to add a bottom covering of sand or peat if the pupae of some Lepidoptera require it. Adult Lepidoptera, especially silk moths (Saturniidae), can be confined in peat pots and will oviposit directly on the walls - the larvae can then be cultured in the same pot or the eggs masses can be cut out and placed in another container. Antlion larvae, or doodlebugs, thrive in peat pots filled with sand in which to build their characteristic pitfalls.

Hunting spiders, such as tarantulas and wolf spiders, do well in peat pots. Spiders with small webs, such as members of the family Linyphiidae, are also suitable. Scorpions can be reared in larger peat containers, but care must be taken to provide an adequate cover. The same advice applied to whipscorpions, harvestmen (daddy-long-legs), millipedes and centipedes.

Some insects are not suitable for peat culture, however. Paper and other large wasps tend to chew through the wall. Large grasshoppers, large crickets, and katydids have mandible which can cut through the thinner peat pots, but not the ones with thicker sides. Termites, of course, are best left in glass or tin. The same is true of ants that nest in wood.

One disadvantage, when compared to glass of plastic, is the fact that peat is not transparent and behavior cannot be observed as well. This can be corrected by cutting a hole in the side and covering it with cellophane, screen or gauze.

Peat pots are available from most mailorder seed companies. Larger sizes, up to 24" in diameter can often be purchased at local garden centers. Be sure to rinse pots before using because sometimes fertilizers are sprayed on the pots to encourage plant growth. Ask for unsprayed pots whenever possible.

Disposable Insect Cages

If you find yourself in the situation where temporary, disposable insect cages would come in handy, here's examples of several possibilities.

Milk carton cage. You will need 2 plastic milk jugs (both the same size), 4 plastic straws, 1/4 yard nylon netting or tulle (preferably white), scissors, masking tape, marking pen and ruler. Draw a line three inches from the bottom of one of the milk jugs, around the entire circumference. Draw a line one inch from the bottom of the other milk jug. Cut the milk jugs along the lines and discard the top portion of each carton. The three inch piece will be the bottom of the cage and the one inch piece will be the top. Next, slit the straws 3/4" at one end. Insert the slits into the corners of the three inch milk jug bottom. Fasten the ends with masking tape. Check to see if the tops of the four straws are all the same height above the table. If not, cut them so they are the same height. If you are using half gallon containers, you may want to trim several inches off the straws anyway, so that the cage is not too tall for its diameter. Slit the tops of the straws 3/4" so that the slits are oriented in the same direction as the slits on the bottom of the straws. This is important, or the top of the cage won't fit on properly. Slip the cage roof (the one inch milk jug piece) into the slits. You may have to adjust the slits so that the roof is level with the table. Use the masking tape to hold the straws in place. You now have a cage top and bottom connected by four plastic straw pillars.

Now all you need to do is cover the sides. Cut a rectangular piece of netting that is at least one inch taller than the straws, and as long as the circumference of the cage bottom plus one side. Starting at one bottom corner, tape the netting around the bottom of the cage. The last 3 to 6 inches will overlap the fist 3 to 6 inches that you taped. When the bottom is securely in place, tape the top edge of the netting to the roof of the cage, starting with the inner corner where you started taping on the bottom. If the overlapped netting forms a gap, use a piece of masking tape to keep the netting closed. When you are ready to add insects to the cage, push them through the sleeve created by the overlapped netting.

If you wish, before taping the netting to the cage you may want to fill the bottom with soil, sand, pebbles, sod, branches, or any other objects that insects might like to use. Paper towels moistened with water or sugar-water can also be added to keep the insects alive.

Numerous variations on this theme are possible. Plastic cellophane wrap (punched with small holes) might also work, as long as you don't leave the cage in the sun. Plastic refrigerator containers, bowls, paper plates, or plastic petri dishes can also be used for cage tops and bottoms.

Tuna can bug cage. The cage described and illustrated on page 10 will also work as a temporary or portable bug cage. In this case you simply omit the plaster of Paris and accessories. The natural tendency of the rolled screen (or acetate) to expand against the edge of the cans will keep the cage together for as long as you need to use it.

Pop bottle bug cages. Clear plastic pop bottles can be fashioned into many types of insect cages with just a little bit of modification. The typical pop bottle can actually be separated into four distinct components, with a little help from a razor blade or scissors. The top portion is just like a funnel, the middle section is a cylinder, the bottom portion is a dome (or bowl), and the black base provides support and stability (or can be discarded). By cutting the bottle in slightly different places you can create a short funnel or a tall funnel, a short cylinder or a tall cylinder, a short dome or a tall dome, and a cage with or without a support base! Using one or more bottles, you can use these various components to create all kinds of bug cages, including a tall cylinder with intact bottom and a dome lid, a tall cylinder without a bottom and a with dome lid (to place over potted plants), or a mini-aquarium/terrarium (inverted dome set in top of cylinder). With a little imagination you can probably create many other innovative bug cages from plastic pop bottles.

Potted Plants

This is a very simple, yet effective method. Bring a potted hostplant into the house or screen patio, put some newspapers down around it to catch the frass, and place your larvae onto the plant.

By using this method, you can keep your bugs at a more constant temperature and still give them the benefit of a living hostplant. They can be moved easily to whatever microhabitat in your house you want them in and you don't have to fuss with netting, cages or cleaning boxes. There is usually little or no problem with disease because the bugs have a nice open air environment and can be given some sunlight if desired. They are also out where you can see them regularly and monitor their progress.

As usual, this technique is not perfect and has a few problems. The first being that a rather unsightly mess of frass and leaf bits can begin to collect on the floor around the hostplant. Another concern is larvae with the wanderlust. Usually the larvae stay on the plant, but there always seem to be a few that go exploring. These individuals are prime candidates for becoming floor stains. There are also household predators to worry about. You might occasionally lose a few larvae to spiders that were either in the house or hitched a ride on the plant. The only other problem is species that burrow when they are ready to pupate. They will usually forgo the soil in the pot and head off into the far reaches of the house. Keep a close eye on them or rear them in a contained method when they are nearing full size.

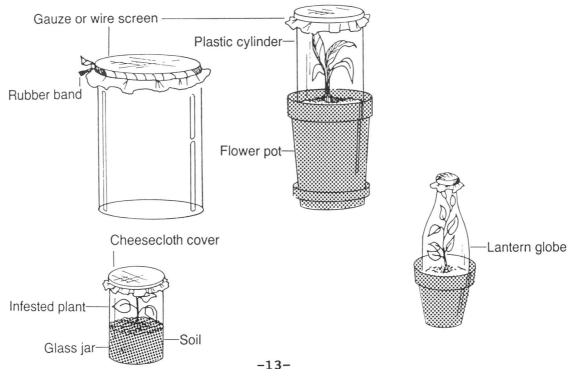

Gauze or wire screen

Rubber band

Plastic cylinder

Flower pot

Cheesecloth cover

Infested plant

Glass jar

Soil

Lantern globe

Sleeves

This is probably the most common method of rearing used today. A rearing sleeve usually consists of a piece of material like fiberglass screen, muslin, or even an old curtain that has been sewn into a tube. This tube is then pulled over a branch and tied off at both ends. Be sure to shake the branch before you put the sleeve on to help knock off some of the predators! Also, unless you have plenty of larvae to spare, don't place larvae in a sleeve until they are second instar or later. This will help reduce mortality by making them too big for some of the smaller predators that lurk in the great outdoors.

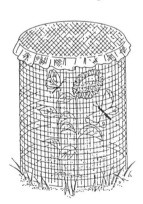 This tried and true method has a well deserved reputation. It is low maintenance, requiring little time. In many cases you only need to put the sleeve out once and the larvae will go to maturity without any further attention. The larvae also gain the benefit of feeding on living hostplant. This often results in larger and healthier adults. Disease is not usually a problem and the larvae receive close to natural conditions. You will probably also have better luck rearing large numbers of larvae to maturity in this manner.

Unfortunately, the sleeve is not without its problems. There is a much higher risk of losing stock to parasites and predators. You may lose livestock to ants, spiders, lacewing larvae, birds, assassin bugs, wasps and assorted parasites, just to name a few. You might even lose lost larvae in sleeves to the most dreaded predator of all - the neighborhood kids!!! You may also not be able to rear some exotic or non native species if the weather in your area is not acceptable to them.

Another problem with sleeves that is rarely brought out into the open is their general appearance. To be blunt, they look like tree condoms. Young rearers living with their parents and advised to get a parental OK; those who don't live at home any more will only have to deal with the neighbors!

Cages

Cages constructed of lightweight wood or aluminum and covered with screening make the great all-around rearing cages. The aluminum stock manufactured for do-it-yourself window screens is especially handy for constructing inexpensive, lightweight, homemade rearing cages.

Outdoor cages can be constructed around shrubs or small trees, and these will yield much the same results as sleeves. They don't need to be changed as often and they usually provide the larvae with an even more natural environment. It is very easy to rear several larvae to maturity in a cage without ever having to move it. These cages pose a few problems not encountered with sleeves though. They need to be anchored to the ground very securely so that they are not blown over by the wind. Raising species that burrow when they are ready to pupate can be a real problem. They can dig right out from under the cage and escape or bury themselves so deep that you can't find them. Some people advocate leaving the cage in place until the adults hatch. This is fine if they are going to hatch before winter comes, but in many areas a cage is unlikely to withstand a severe winter unless it was extremely well constructed. Cages can also be a real pain in the "rear-ing" to sterilize.

Terraria and Aquaria

Standard glass terraria/aquaria can be used for rearing many types of arthropods, including both aquatic and terrestrial species. Gallon jars, battery jars, and fish bowls can be used in much the same way as the larger aquaria/terraria.

Because of the limited air circulation, these glass containers work best for insects and other arthropods requiring either moist conditions or extremely warm, dry conditions. NEVER put a glass container filled with insect livestock in direct sunlight! The resulting heat build up will be fatal.

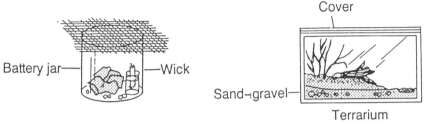

MAINTAINING AN OPTIMAL TEMPERATURE

Many insects need to be kept warmer than room temperature, so you will need to supply the localized heat necessary to keep them warm and healthy. It may be possible to keep your livestock in a small room, or a specially constructed cabinet, that can be kept warm more economically. Otherwise, ordinary incandescent light bulbs can often be used. Some insects are adversely affected by the bright light; in this case infrared heat lamps can provide heat without all the white light. If you use lightbulbs for heat, especially the infrared kind, check your livestock frequently for signs of dehydration and take corrective measures as necessary. You must also make sure that the insects cannot come into direct contact with any hot bulbs. Some types of heaters, such as heat cables and heat pads (which are available from garden centers and pet shops), can also be used to gently warm containers from the bottom.

SHELTERS AND SUBSTRATES FOR YOUR LIVESTOCK

Whenever possible you should provide your livestock with suitable shelter(s) within your containers. Shelters are important as they provide hiding and resting places and provide localized refuges with higher temperature and humidity levels. Shelters may be as simple as a piece of crumpled tissue paper or paper toweling, or as elaborate as a "critter condo" made out of cardboard egg cartons. Drink cup caddies (like the ones you get a fast food establishments) make excellent shelters when turned upside down. Plants (live or imitation), curved bark, hollowed out log sections, or stones also work well (and look more natural).

Burrowing species should be provided with an ample amount of soft substrate. Sand, potting soil, humus, sawdust, and peat moss work well, but many breeders prefer vermiculite because it is inorganic, sterile and lightweight. Non-burrowing terrestrial species can be given a substrate of ground corncob, bark mulch, aquarium gravel, or dust-free kitty litter.

FEEDING YOUR INSECTS

Your insects will require a constant supply of high quality food. Plant eating insects will need a fresh supply of foliage from their host plants. **VERY IMPORTANT: Whenever you gather foliage or other plant materials to feed to your livestock, be absolutely certain that it has not been treated with pesticides or contaminated in any way! Fruits and vegetables purchased at the grocery store or picked from the garden should be thoroughly washed before being fed to your livestock. These preventive measures could very well save the lives of your livestock!**

Predatory insects need live prey. This means you'll either have to culture a colony of acceptable prey insects or collect live insects from outdoors. You can simplify this task by using insect-collecting traps (pitfall, blacklight, Malaise, windowpane, etc.) to gather insects. You can also collect leaf litter samples and run them through Berlese funnels to sort out living insects. Be careful with household insects, as they could be contaminated with toxic substances! If you raise crickets to feed to your insects, make sure to feed them some flaked fish food in addition to the vegetable matter to increase their protein content.

Many other insects can be reared on commonly available food items such as dog food, powdered milk, vegetables, honey, flour, bread, and/or food scraps.

Specific food recommendations for various insects can be found throughout this manual.

ARTIFICIAL DIETS FOR INSECT LIVESTOCK

Some insects can be reared with artificial diets, and this greatly simplifies the task of feeding insect livestock especially when you have lots of individuals. Some artificial diets are composed of readily available substances and you should be able to make these yourself. A few recipes for diets are given so that you can experiment with their use in your own rearing projects. Other diets are more complex and will need to be purchased from commercial sources (see Appendix A).

1. General insect diet*:
   Ingredients A: corn flour .... 4 parts (by weight, not volume)
                  whole wheat flour ..... 2 parts
                  skim milk powder ...... 2 parts
                  dried powdered yeast .. 1 part
                  wheat bran .... 2 parts
       Mix the above ingredients thoroughly and store in a large pest-proof container.

   Ingredients B: honey (1 part) plus glycerin (1 part)
       Mix equal parts of ingredients A and B (by weight). Let the mixture stand for at least 24 hours before using (so the liquids can be absorbed). Keep the finished mixture refrigerated.
   (* - Successfully used with wax moths, saw-toothed grain beetle, Indian meal moth, many dermestid beetles and grasshoppers.)

2. Artificial Diet for General Lepidoptera Larvae:
   Ingredients A: agar .... 25 g
                  water .... 1200 ml
   Heat the agar and water together (stirring continuously) until it is just ready to boil. It should begin to foam when ready.

Ingredients B: brewer's yeast ....120 g
                ascorbic acid .... 12 g (Vitamin C)
                methylparaben .... 9 g (fungicide)
                sorbic acid .... 3 g (fungicide)
                dried lima beans .... 1200 g (soaked overnight)
                water .... 1000 ml

Put the above ingredients into a blender while the agar and water solution is heating. Run the blender for 1-2 minutes. When the agar solution is ready pour it into the blender and run the blender for a few minutes. The mixture does not need to be completely smooth. Pour the hot mixture directly into containers. Do not wait long before pouring because it will begin to set-up almost immediately. Allow it to stand in the containers for 2-3 hours before capping.

3. Artificial Diet for Smaller Moth Larvae:
     Ingredients A: pinto/navy beans .... 604 g (soaked weight)
                    brewer's yeast .... 100 g
                    sorbic acid (dry) .... 3 g
                    ascorbic acid (dry) ..... 10 g (Vitamin C)
                    tegosept .... 6 g (may be omitted)
                    formaldehyde .... 6 ml
                    water .... 1120 ml
     Ingredients B: agar .... 40 g
                    water (boiling) .... 800 ml

Mix all the dry ingredients except the agar and place them and the beans (which have been soaked overnight) into a blender. Add the 1120 ml of water and blend for 10 minutes. Slowly add agar to 800 ml of boiling water, stirring constantly until it becomes transparent and thickens. Add agar mixture gradually to the mix in the blender. Add the formaldehyde. Blend 2 more minutes. Pour into small paper cups and refrigerate. Let the diet reach room temperature before feeding to larvae.
This formula is mostly for small species and is not intended for egg production (they generally won't hatch). The same mix with 143 g of wheat germ added is better for some species.

4. Artificial Diet for Silkmoth Larvae:
     Ingredients A: agar .... 25 g
                    water .... 840 ml
     Ingredients B: salts, Wesson .... 10 g
                    sucrose .... 35 g
                    wheat germ .... 30 g
                    casein, vitamin free .... 35 g
                    alphacel .... 5 g (powdered cellulose)
                    cholesterol .... 0.5 g (or beta-sitosterol)
                    formaldehyde .... 1 ml (37%)
                    inhibitor solution ...... 20 ml
                    10% KOH .... 10 ml
     Ingredients 3: aureomycin .... 2.5 g
                    kanamycin sulfate ..... 0.14 g
                    ascorbic acid .... 4 g
                    choline chloride 1g
                    inositol .... 0.15 g
                    linseed oil .... 1 ml
                    vitamin suspension .... 2 ml

The inhibitor solution consists of 40g ascorbic acid and 30g methyl-hydroxyl-benzoate dissolved in 340ml 95% ethanol.

The vitamin suspension consists of 0.12mg biotin, 6mg calcium pantothenate, 1.5mg folic acid, 6mg niacinamide, 1.5mg pyridoxine hydrochloride, 3ml thiamine hydrochoride and 0.012mg vitamin B_{12} per milliliter.

The agar is dissolved in boiling water and blended with the ingredients from list A. The vitamins and antibiotics (list B) are added and blended after cooling to 50°C. This mixture is poured into a beaker for solidification and then transferred to polyethylene bags for storage at 2°C.

This diet works well for Hyalophora cecropia and H. gloveri, as well as for Samia cynthia when the inositol, which is not necessary for H. cecropia, is present. The diet **does not** work well for Antherea polyphemus and A. pernyi.

WATERING YOUR INSECTS

Most insect cultures need an ample supply of clean drinking water to ensure their successful growth and development. Several ways to provide water to your insects are outlined below. All of the methods are easy to use and require a minimum of maintenance. However, it is very important to always keep any "drinking fountains" clean and mold-free.

Vertical Fountain. Fill a tall, slender glass or plastic jar with clean water. Place several layers of cheesecloth over the jar opening and secure it with an elastic band. Turn the jar upside down in a shallow dish or on a flat piece of glass or plastic. The insects will drink from the absorbent material, which will also prevent them from drowning.

Horizontal Fountain. Use a slender jar, test tube, or large vial with a lid or cork big enough to fit the container's opening. Bore a hole in the lid or cork and insert a dental wick, roll of absorbent cotton or similar material into the lid or cork. (If the container has a smaller diameter you can often plug the complete opening with the absorbent material, thus eliminating the need for the cork.) For maximum access to all the water in the vial, fill the jar or vial with clean water and lay it on its side in the rearing cage. The insects will drink from the moist wick.

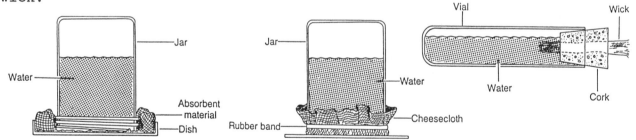

Insect Watering Devices

Water Dish. Larger insects can be given water in a shallow dish (plastic jar lid, petri dish, or furniture floor guard). The floor guards work exceptionally well because they are thick and not prone to tipping.

Misting. Other types of insects can be watered by periodically misting the cage and foodplants with water. Many types of household and plant misters are available, and be absolutely certain that any mister you use is free of contaminants, toxic substances and pesticides before you use it! You can also make a homemade sprinkler bottle by obtaining any suitable bottle with a soft plastic lid that can be punctured with a small nail.

PREVENTING DISEASES AND PEST INFESTATIONS

Controlling the environmental conditions within your rearing containers will in great part determine the frequency and severity of outbreaks of fungal, viral and bacterial diseases among your insect livestock. Avoid excess moisture at all times since this promotes disease outbreak, especially if excess leftover food and excess frass is not removed on a regular basis. Overcrowding livestock also frequently leads to disease outbreak (and when disease does break out it spreads more rapidly).

If you experience a disease outbreak, inspect all livestock carefully and destroy any that do not appear completely healthy. Rearing containers and equipment should be sterilized. This can be accomplished with boiling water or with a bleach solution. Mix one gallon of water with 3/4 cup bleach. Wash and soak the items for at least 2 to 5 minutes, and then rinse thoroughly with clean (preferably distilled) water and let air dry.

Some parasites, predators and scavengers may invade your cultures from time to time. Check all incoming foliage for hitchhiking predators and parasites. Scavengers, like dermestid beetles and ants, are attracted to moisture and leftover food, so keep your cages free of waste food. Keeping containers fitted with a lid (cloth, screen or solid) will also help to repel unwanted pests. It is generally NOT a good idea to use any insecticides around your livestock! If nuisance scavengers are getting in, try ringing the table legs with petroleum jelly, or place the cage on "stilts" in a large pan of water (to act as a protective moat).

SOURCES OF REARING EQUIPMENT AND SUPPLIES

One of the nice things about insect rearing is that much of the equipment and supplies you might need can be found around the house, or can be fashioned from inexpensive materials found around the house. However, every once in a while you might run into an item or supply that you'll want to purchase, either out of necessity or convenience. Some rearing materials are available from organizations like the Young Entomologists' Society (call or write for a catalog), or from commercial enterprises. The best and most complete source of information on where you can purchase rearing supplies can be found in "The Insect Study Sourcebook" by Gary A. Dunn (see bibliography).

SOURCES OF INFORMATION AND ADVICE

From time to time you may need to seek advice from expert insect rearers. Many rearers publish helpful information in scientific and entomological journals (see suggestions on page 4), and the answers to your questions may often be found in these articles. (Don't forget to check the bibliography at the end of this manual.)

You can personally observe insect cultures at insect zoos and butterfly houses that are located in many cities around the United States and Canada. The best and most complete source of information on these facilities can be found in "The Insect Study Sourcebook" by Gary A. Dunn (see bibliography). "Insect zoos" are usually located at nature centers, natural history museums, zoos, and parks, so you might want to inquire at any facilities in your area. In many cases the curator (caretaker) of the insect livestock would be more than happy to assist you with insect rearing questions and problems, and will probably even give you a "behind the scenes" tour of the facility (when advance notice is given).

PART II: INSECT REARING

AQUATIC INSECTS

Background Information

As the largest group of animals, the insects occupy practically every type of watery (aquatic) habitat. There are insects that live in, on, or near both fresh water and saltwater, including some ocean surfaces, salt marshes, salt lakes, mineral springs, puddles, alpine pools, roadside ditches, tree holes, pitcher plant leaves, freshwater marshes, swamps, pond and lakes, underground streams in caves, brooks, creeks, streams and rivers. Only the ocean depths and the deepest freshwater lakes are void of insects.

Some of the insect orders are completely aquatic, spending at least one stage of their life in the water. The common "aquatic orders" include the mayflies (Ephemeroptera), dragonflies and damselflies (Odonata), stoneflies (Plecoptera), and caddisflies (Trichoptera). Other insect orders contain one or more families that are aquatic or semi-aquatic for all, or part, of their life. For example, in the springtails (Collembola) there are several families with aquatic species. In the true bugs (Hemiptera) there are water boatmen, backswimmers, marsh treaders, water striders, ripple bugs, giant water bugs, waterscorpions, velvet water bugs, creeping water bugs, and toad bugs. In the Neuroptera there are spongilla flies (they live inside freshwater sponges), dobsonflies, fishflies, and alderflies. In the beetles (Coleoptera) there are crawling water beetles, whirlygigs, predaceous diving beetles, burrowing water beetles, water scavenger beetles, water penny beetles, mud-loving beetles, long-toed water beetles, and riffle beetles. In the true flies (Diptera) there are mosquitoes, midges, black flies, crane flies, snipe flies, hover flies, and shore flies. There are even some moths (Order Lepidoptera)

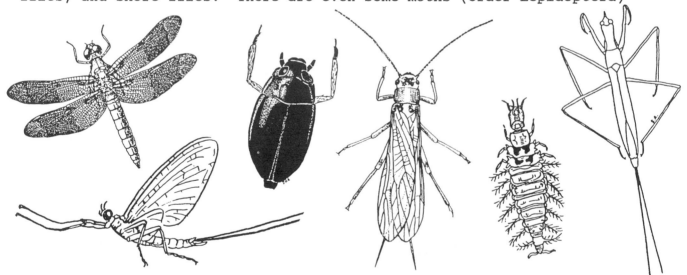

There are two major problems with an aquatic lifestyle: methods of locomotion and sources of air (oxygen). There are actually two different problems associated with locomotion, namely, staying put in swiftly moving water and moving about in still water! Insects that inhabit swiftly flowing waters use a variety of "anchors" to stay in one place. They may use their claws as hooks, glue themselves to rocks, use suction cups, or hold themselves down with pebbles or sticks. Insects that live in still waters move around by swimming with legs shaped like paddles, wiggling their bodies, or shooting spurts of water out of their hind end.

The ways in which aquatic insects get their air for breathing depends on where they live. Insects that live on the surface of the water generally have no problem getting air. Those insects that live near the surface, but spend lots of time swimming beneath the surface of the water, may use special breathing tubes ("snorkling") or carry an air bubble trapped around the outside of the body ("scuba diving"). Some insects spend all of their time under water and they are able to take dissolved oxygen right out of the water with tracheal gills.

Rearing Instructions

Aquatic insects can be collected from any pond, river, stream, roadside ditch or woodland pool. A variety of insects are easily maintained in aquaria and many different kinds can often be kept in the same container. Collect the insects with an aquatic dip net and transport them in a loosely covered container. Those insects like water striders, water boatmen, backswimmers, and diving beetles that breathe by "scuba diving" (plastron respiration) should be transported in a container filled with wet, crumpled paper towels. Do not transport them in water-filled containers. The wave action in the container will watersoak their oxygen-laden body hairs, making it difficult for them to breathe. If your aquatic insects do become waterlogged, simply dry them on paper towelling for a few minutes to restore the hairs' effectiveness. Those insects which breathe with gills (for example, dragonflies, damselflies, mayflies and stoneflies) should be transported directly in water.

The fall is a good time to collect aquatic insects. Many aquatic insects, unlike their terrestrial relatives, remain active throughout the winter months. An aquarium full of aquatic insects will provide many hours of observation and study during the fall and winter.

Aquatic insects which are relatively easy to rear include the dragonflies and damselflies (Odonata), mayflies (Ephemeroptera), stoneflies (Plecoptera), water bugs (Hemiptera), mosquitoes (Diptera), diving beetles (Coleoptera), and caddisflies (Trichoptera). The techniques for rearing aquatic insects are a little different from those used for terrestrial insects. You can use any watertight container for rearing aquatic insects, but if you use a glass jar or aquarium you'll be able to see the insects. Large, wide-mouth jars, fishbowls, and aquaria all work well. Spread a 1-inch layer of <u>clean</u> (thoroughly washed!) gravel in the bottom of the container and fill with clean pond water or other unchlorinated water (let tap water stand for 24 hours or buy distilled water at the grocery store, which will also eliminate chemical/mineral buildup associated with hard water). You can add some aquatic plants, sticks and/or stones (obtained from a pond, stream or pet store). The plants provide food and hiding places, and give off oxygen needed by the insects. Don't worry too much about algal growth, because many insects can use algae as food. If the algae gets out of hand a few snails will perform the necessary housekeeping chores. Some insects require an abundance of dissolved oxygen in the water, so use a bubbler. A filter may also help keep the tank cleaner, but will not replace the need to scoop out larger pieces of uneaten food and waste products. If the water becomes too cloudy, you may change up to 1/4 of the water every two weeks. You may also want to have a screen top for the aquarium, to keep emerging adults from escaping.

<u>Food</u>. Many aquatic insects are predaceous, which means they feed on other insects or microscopic water animals. If you fill the aquarium with pond water instead of bottled water, your insects will often get enough to eat. Tadpoles, minnows, guppies and crickets serve as food sources for giant water bugs, predaceous diving beetles (and their larvae, known as "water tigers"), and dragonfly nymphs. Dragonfly nymphs are easily caught

in roadside ditches, ponds and weedy lake margins. When the nymphs are small, the best food will be other aquatic insects. Water boatmen, backswimmers, and small beetles can be netted and placed in the aquarium to serve as prey for the dragonfly nymphs. Other crustaceans, small pollywogs (tadpoles), and even small fish will be suitable as the nymphs grow. Many times, however, it is inconvenient or impossible to search for these various food species several times each week. In such a case meat from your own dinner table will be acceptable to larger nymphs. Raw hamburger, baloney (bologna), hot dogs, bits of cold, roast chicken will be eaten by dragonfly nymphs if properly presented. The meat must be broken into small fragments and waved one at a time in front of each nymph on a piece of thin wire. The nymphs will strike the meat and then the wire must be dislodged without scaring the nymph. Take care not to touch the nymph with the food lest you scare it. Rather, wave the food slowly about 1/3" from its eye and let it approach and seize the meat. An element of learning seems to be involved here because one nymph may learn that the meat is good to eat and take 3 or 4 pieces in succession, whereas another may be scared by the initial contact with the meat and subsequently refuse to eat any.

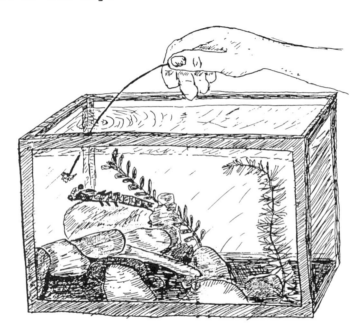

A method for feeding aquatic predatory insects

     Mosquito larvae will eat finely crushed dog biscuits or powdered milk. The tiniest pinch of either is enough to feed many mosquito larvae.
     Some aquatic insect food (like decaying leaves) can be gathered in the fall before the ground freezes and stored for use during the winter. Live insects can be reared or purchased at pet supply stores.

Table 1: Food Suggestions for Aquatic Insects

Insect	Food habits	Possible foods
Damselfly nymphs	carnivores	bloodworms and small crustaceans (Daphnia, Cyclops, ostrocods)
dragonfly nymphs	carnivores	small crustaceans at first; pieces of worms and tadpoles for mature nymphs
stonefly nymphs	herbivores	moist decaying leaves
water striders	scavengers	flies, leafhoppers and soft-bodied insects
backswimmers	carnivores	mosquito larvae and ostracods
water scorpions	carnivores	ground beetles, freshwater shrimps, mosquito larvae, small insects of all sorts
mosquitoes	herbivores	protozoa-hay infusions plus yeast
whirlygig beetles	scavengers	dead insects on bits of raw meat floating on water's surface
water scavenger beetle	scavenger	decaying plant or animal matter, leaves and algae

HOUSE AND FIELD CRICKETS

Background Information

The length of time it takes crickets to complete their development depends on several factors: temperature, moisture, freedom (amount of space), and the presence of any disease-causing organisms, predators, or parasites.

If all other conditions are favorable, the developmental time is most directly regulated by temperature. Nymphs held at 90° F. may require only 30 to 35 days to complete development, while those held at 80° F may require up to 65 days to mature. Four hundred crickets can be reared every 3 months in a container as small as 24 inches in diameter. A smaller container will result in fewer crickets being produced.

Both the black field cricket (<u>Gryllus</u> species) and the tan house cricket (<u>Acheta domestica</u>) can be reared successfully. House crickets are readily obtained from pet supply houses and "cricket farms".

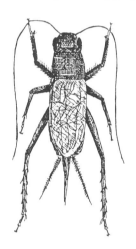 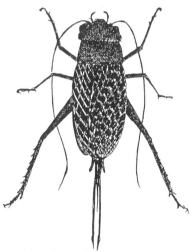

House cricket (<u>Acheta domestica</u>)   Field cricket (<u>Gryllus</u> species)

Rearing Instructions

Prepare a suitable cage for your crickets. The cage can be a large glass jar (with a screen or cloth covering), metal can, or a screen cage. If you use a glass container it helps to treat the inside, upper portion of the jar with a very thin layer of mineral oil, petroleum jelly, or furniture wax to keep the crickets from escaping. Spread 3 or 4 inches of dry, clean sand in the bottom of each cage.

Place a small plastic or glass container of moist sand in the cage so that the top edge is about 1/2 inch above the dry sand. This container is the egg laying site, and must be kept moist, but not wet, at all times. As an alternative you can accomplish the same thing by sloping the sand 20-30 degrees from one side of the container to the other. Moisten the sand at the lower end of the slope with water. Some cricket "farmers" prefer to have separate egg laying containers. They fill coffee cans with damp sand and then place 20 to 30 adult crickets (half males and half females) in each can. The female cricket is readily distinguished by her long ovipositor. The sand is moistened once and then not again for 3 months. The young crickets (nymphs) must have dry sand to remain disease-free, so once hatching begins to occur the cricket nymphs need to be moved to drier quarters.

The small container of moist sand, or the separate egg-laying containers, must be kept warm (80-90° F) during the incubation period. Eggs will begin to hatch within 3 weeks after they've been laid. The newly-hatched nymphs are very tiny and blend in with the sand. You'll need to look very carefully to see them.

Hiding Places. You must provide places for your crickets to hide. Paper or foam egg cartons work very well. You can also use folded corrugated cardboard, excelsior, or hay. Young cricket nymphs must be kept separate from the adults until they are one-third to one-half grown, or they are likely to be eaten! After they have reached the required size, they may be safely put in with the adults.

Food. Very young nymphs require soft food. You can feed them slices of banana or apple, or pulverized dog food (or cat food or rabbit food) laid on pieces of lettuce (wash thoroughly and use only inner leaves that are not likely to be treated with pesticides). Poultry laying mash also works very well. The Purina Company even makes a special Cricket Chow for raising crickets! Place the food in a shallow container with excelsior or hay around it so the crickets have easy access to the food. Placing the food in a dish allows for easier housekeeping. The cage must be kept free of unused food and dead crickets to prevent mold or disease. Adult crickets will do well on crushed dog nuggets or poultry laying mash. If you wish, you can supplement their diet with rolled oats and bits of banana, apple, lettuce, or other pulpy fruits or vegetables.

Water. Crickets must have a constant supply of drinking water. Indeed, the water supply is more important than a constant supply of food. You can make a drinking fountain by placing an inverted jar in a shallow dish. Clean the fountain and replace the absorbent material every month, or as needed.

EASTERN LUBBER GRASSHOPPER
(Romalea guttata)

Background Information
The eastern lubber grasshopper can be collected during the spring and summer along roadsides and other grassy areas in the southeastern United States, especially in the Gulf Coast states. There are two subspecies: one is black with yellow markings and the other is olive green with yellow markings, but the nymphs of both are black and yellow. All stages are rather slow moving and rely on their warning coloration and bad flavor for protection from predators. The adults have reddish wings which are too small for for flight but seem to be used using by males in a defensive behavior against intruders. Nymphs or adults which are collected in the wild occasionally are parasitized or diseased, so it is a good idea to collect a few extra specimens to allow for those that die early.

Rearing Instructions
Adults should be kept in a fairly spacious cage. Cages 20" x 30" x 20" high, containing about 20 grasshoppers, seem to work well. The temperature should be kept about 80°F, and the relative humidity should range between 50 and 80%.

The food for all stages of this grasshopper consists of a mixed diet including garden vegetables such as lettuce, kale, collard greens, carrot slices, sweet potato slices, and apple slices. Wheat, grown in a greenhouse or outside, is especially important early in the growth of the nymphs. With adults wheat may be omitted if supplies run low, however it is nice to have it available in the cage. Garden weeds such as dandelion, plantain, and grass can be used to supplement the diet, but these are not necessary. A tray of dry bran or crushed dry dog food (of a cereal type) should also be available in the cage. A dish of water with a folded paper towel in it should also be present. A layer of sand can be used on the floor of the cage to improve overall appearance and to facilitate cleaning.

An oviposition tray should be placed in the cage with the adults. The pre-oviposition period of mature grasshoppers lasts about four weeks. The oviposition tray which we have found most useful consists of a plastic container (shoe box) 7" x 12" x 3" deep. The container is filled with moist sand. Water should be added at least once a week so that the sand is kept moist, but not flooded. Egg pods (each containing about 15 or 20 eggs) will be deposited in the moist sand, and after about 10 or 12 egg pods have been laid (which may take from several days to 2 weeks) the tray should be removed and replaced. Remove all frass from the surface of the sand to prevent mold.

After the tray has been removed from the cage, a loose fitting lid should be placed on the oviposition tray and it should be put in a location where the temperature can be kept at about 70°F. The tray should be checked at weekly intervals to be certain that the sand is always moist. After about 85 days the temperature should be increased to about 80°F and an empty plastic tray of the same size inverted and taped over the oviposition tray to serve as an emergence cage. Nymphs usually begin to hatch after about 30 days. The tray should be checked every day and the nymphs transferred to small cages about one cubic foot in size. Mortality among newly emerged nymphs is often as high as 40%, but seems to be lower in cages with good ventilation. Nymphs feed mainly on leaves of wheat. If wheat is carefully planted with roots in a dish before being placed into the grasshopper cage, it will stay fresh for several days. The grasshopper nymphs should also be provided with pieces of vegetables, a small dish of bran, and a dish of water as described above. The nymphal stage lasts about two months. Nymphs have greater success during molting if sticks or branches on which they hand are available. Nymphs which molt on the floor of the cage usually end up deformed.

Total length of time for one generation in captivity is about 8 months. In nature the egg pods overwinter, so in captivity eggs could probably be kept dormant for a fair length of time at around 50° or 60°F.

"DOMESTIC" COCKROACHES

Background Information

Cockroaches, also known as waterbugs and palmettobugs, are common household pests. Except for periods of warm weather when they may migrate from house to house, domestic cockroaches in the northern portion of the United States spend their entire life inside buildings. Usually they are found in basements, bathrooms, and kitchens where they feed upon a wide variety of foods, including cereals, sugary foods, meats, cheese, beer and soda pop, as well as leather, bookbindings, and wallpaper paste. They can be carried into homes in cardboard cartons, sacks, beverage containers, furniture, and pet foods.

Cockroaches have long been companions of man. The old Romans called them "lucifuga" because of their habit of running away from light. Most cockroach species are active at night and hide in dark areas during the day. The word cockroach no doubt can be traced to the Spanish word "cucaracha."

The exact origin of our domestic species is disputed, but many are tropical forms and now are widely distributed throughout the world by human commerce. Five different species of cockroaches are most widespread. Four of these are domestic roaches, while the fifth is more at home outdoors but also gets into the house.

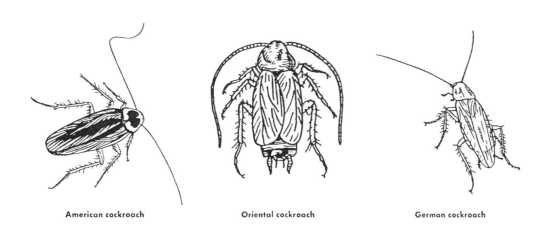

American cockroach   Oriental cockroach   German cockroach

The American cockroach, <u>Periplaneta americana</u> (left), our largest, may grow to 1 1/2 inches (35 mm). It is reddish-brown or mahogany with light markings on top of the thorax (the body division that bears the winds and legs) and matures in about seven months. The adults may live for up to 18 months. The nymphs are grayish-brown, becoming reddish-brown as they mature, and wingless. It prefers damp areas such as basements, and may be found around pipes, sewage systems, and drainage systems in homes, commercial buildings, and greenhouses.

The Oriental cockroach, <u>Blatta orientalis</u> (center), is black, 1 1/4 inches (30 mm) long when full-grown and has short wings, the wings of the female being only rudimentary. It may take as long as 22 months to mature, and is a relatively sluggish insect. It prefers damp, cool areas, especially basements and crawl spaces and near drains and leaky water pipes. They can be found under sinks, refrigerators and washing machines if those areas are damp. Outdoors they can be found beneath decaying leaves and stones, and in mulch, garbage piles, and water-meter vaults.

The German cockroach, <u>Blatella germanica</u> (right), is smaller, slightly over 1/2 inch (12-15 mm) long, brownish-tan with two black parallel lines just behind the head. The nymphs are darker, wingless, and also have two lengthwise stripes behind the head. This species prefers high relative humidity and warmth and is a significant pest problem in homes, restaurants, hotels, food plants, warehouses, dumps, office buildings, hospitals, ships, and retail stores. It is quite active and can easily migrate throughout buildings thus becoming a major pest in apartment buildings. This roach prefers a kitchen or bathroom where there is plenty of food, moisture and hiding places, but they can often be found in other parts of the house as well. This species produces more eggs and has more generations per year (3 or 4) than other cockroaches.

The brown-banded cockroach, <u>Supella longipalpa</u>, is a fairly recent introduction, first found in Florida in 1903. It has since spread throughout the South and is now quite common in some areas of the northern U.S. While it normally congregates, individuals can wander throughout the house, hiding in furniture, bookcases, television sets, radios, computers, light switches, behind pictures hung on the wall, and closets or other

secluded locations, especially those high off the floor. It is slightly
under 1/2 inch (10-12 mm) when mature, and is colored a straw brown. Two
brownish bands are located on the wings of the adult, one where the wings
join the body, and one a little further back toward the wing tips. The
term "brown-banded", however, describes the immature form more accurately
than the adult, since the bands are conspicuous on the abdomens of the
nymphs. The species prefers temperatures over 80°F, and takes up to 150
days to mature at this temperature.

Another common roach in the eastern United States is the Pennsylvania
wood roach, <u>Parcoblatta</u> <u>pennsylvanica</u>. This species lives outdoors and is
not as fast nor wary as its house-dwelling relatives. They may wander
into buildings in wooded areas, or may be brought into the house under the
bark of fireplace wood (they are common in woodpiles), and can exist in
the home, living on food in the kitchen. The males of this species have
long wings and may fly for short distances; indeed, they are often
attracted to porch lights and lighted windows. The females have short
wings and are usually found around houses only in wooded situations. The
adults are about 3/4 to 1 inch (20 - 25 mm) long and are colored a drab
brown. They require one year to mature.

Biology and Life Cycle

Roaches lay their eggs in large numbers within a single capsule
(ootheca) which contains from 12 to 32 eggs, depending on the species.
The egg compartments within the capsule are indicated by grooves on the
outside. The egg capsules range in color from dark brown to tannish brown
and are somewhat bean-shaped. They are usually deposited in out-of-the-
way places such as on the underside of shelves, inside cupboard corners,
bottoms of drawers, and similar hard-to-see areas. Egg capsules from
which the eggs have hatched will float, while those that have unhatched
eggs will usually sink in water. The nymphs grow slowly, requiring 2 to
18 months to complete their development.

Rearing Instructions

Any type of cage or solid container covered with a screen lid will
work well for rearing domestic cockroaches. Apply a thin layer of
petroleum jelly to the inside rim of the container to prevent those
roaches that congregate at the top from escaping when the cover is off.
Some absorbent material, such as sand, sawdust, vermiculite, or ground
corncob, should be placed in the bottom of the cage. This material should
be replaced every 4 to 6 months. Pour the used material through a sieve
to avoid throwing away any small nymphs or egg capsules (oothecae). Do
not remove the hatched egg capsules from the cages, as they afford hiding
places for the young nymphs and a source of food. Place a small number of
cardboard containers (paper towel rolls, egg cartons, or drink caddies) in
the cage for hiding and resting places. To produce the maximum number of
hiding places, these items should be bundled together into "apartment
houses" with rubber bands or glue. Place the cage in a warm location, at
least 70° to 80° F. Also, the roaches prefer subdued light, so don't
keep them in an area with bright lights (and don't use a light bulb to
warm them unless absolutely necessary).

<u>Food</u>. Any high-protein dry dog food (do not use commercial guinea pig
or rabbit food!) can be a staple in your roaches' diet. Dog food can be
fed directly from the package, no pulverizing is necessary. If you see
evidence of "wing-nipping" (a tendency towards cannibalism), you can
safely assume that your roaches' diet is protein deficient. Supplement
their diet with protein-rich foods such as powdered milk, meat scraps,
fresh liver, or flaked fish food to eliminate this problem. The protein

diet should also be supplemented with fresh fruits and vegetables (lettuce, carrots, celery tops, apples, or potatoes), bran, wheat germ, or bread.

Water. A supply of drinking water is important for roach survival. If necessary, use a "drinking fountain" to provide water to the roaches. If you feed your roaches lots of fresh lettuce, apples or potatoes, which are high in moisture, the need for a separate supply of drinking water will be less critical.

GIANT COCKROACHES
(Blaberus spp.)

Background Information
The Blaberus cockroach is a giant among roaches, measuring up to 3 inches in length and 1.5 inches in width (depending on the species). These roaches are not native to the northern United States; they are found in Florida, the Caribbean, and Central and South America. These insects are easy to rear and observe, and are well-suited to experimentation.

Since these roaches are not native to most parts of the USA, you will probably have to purchase them from a biological supply house. Because Blaberus roaches are potential household pests, a USDA permit is required to have them mailed to you. The supply house will assist you with this.

Biology and Life Cycle
Nymphs. The youngest Blaberus nymphs bear little resemblance to the adults. When they first appear they are about 1/4-inch long and quite flat. The nymphs grow fairly rapidly through 7 - 8 stages, each separated by a molt. Wings appear after the last molt (when the roach becomes an adult). The average time required for development, from the first nymphal stage to adulthood, is a little less than 6 months.

Adults. Adult male and female Blaberus roaches look very much alike, but can be distinguished by close observation. To identify the sex of a Blaberus roach, grasp the roach with your thumb pressed against the underside of the thorax. Examine the underside of the last abdominal segment. Both sexes have a conspicuous pair of appendages (cerci) projecting from the outer margins of the last segment. The males also have a second pair of appendages (styli). The styli are very small and are located just inside of the cerci.

The female produces egg capsules (oothecae). A Blaberus ootheca is about 1/2 inch long and contains 20+ compartments, each with an egg. Most other roach species deposit the capsules long before egg hatch; not so in Blaberus. The oothecae are rarely seen because the females hold them within their bodies, where they eventually hatch. Thus it appears the females gives "live birth" to 20 or more young nymphs.

Rearing Instructions
Any type of cage covered with ordinary window screen will work well for rearing these roaches. Even the smallest nymphs are too large to squeeze through the mesh. Some absorbent material, such as sand, sawdust vermiculite, or ground corncob, should be placed in the bottom of the cage. This material should be replaced every 4 to 6 months. Pour the used material through a sieve to avoid throwing away any small nymphs or egg capsules. These are tropical insects, so place the cage in a warm location. They seem to do best at about 80° F. Also, the roaches

prefer subdued light, so don't keep them in an area with bright lights (and don't use a light bulb to warm them unless absolutely necessary).

Food. Any high-protein dry dog food can be a staple in your roaches' diet. Dog food can be fed directly from the package, no pulverizing is necessary. If you see evidence of "wing-nipping" (a tendency towards cannibalism), you can safely assume that your roaches' diet is protein deficient. Supplement their diet with protein-rich foods such as powdered milk, meat scraps or fresh liver to eliminate this problem. The protein diet should also be supplemented with fresh fruits or vegetables such as lettuce, carrots, celery tops, apples or potatoes. The apples and potatoes are high in moisture and may eliminate the need for a separate supply of drinking water.

Water. A supply of drinking water is important for roach survival. If necessary, use a "drinking fountain" to provide water to the roaches.

MADAGASCAR HISSING COCKROACH
(Gromphadorina portentosa)

Background Information
The Madagascar hissing cockroach is a large species of roach, measuring up to 2.5 inches in length and 1 inch in width when mature. These roaches are not native to North America; they are found on the island of Madagascar in the Indian Ocean, off the eastern coast of Africa. These roaches are easy to rear and observe.

These roaches are unusual in their ability to produce an audible hissing sound when disturbed. This defensive mechanism is made possible by rapidly forcing air out of the first abdominal trachea and spiracle by contracting the abdomen. In captivity, older adults soon adapt to frequent handling and rarely hiss unless left undisturbed for a long period of time. Younger adults are almost always more "vocal".

Since these roaches are not native to the USA, you will have to purchase them from a biological supply house, or a local pet store. Because these roaches are potential household pests, a USDA or state permit may be required to have them mailed to you. The supply house will usually handle this for you.

Biology and Life Cycle
Nymphs. The youngest nymphs bear little resemblance to the adults. When they first appear they are about 1/4-inch long and quite flat. The nymphs grow fairly rapidly through 7 - 8 stages, each separated by a molt. Wings are always lacking, even in the adult stage. The average time required for development, from the first nymphal stage to adulthood, is a little less than 10 months.

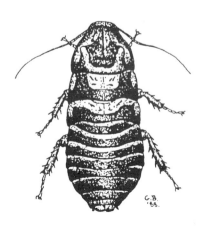

Adults. Adult male and female hissing roaches look very much alike. The female hissing cockroach produces egg capsules (oothecae), but retains them within the outer portion of the reproductive tract until they are ready to hatch. The ootheca of this roach is whitish and about 1/4 inch long and contains many compartments, each with an egg. The oothecae are rarely seen because the females hold them within their bodies, where they eventually hatch. Thus it appears the females gives "live birth" to 20 or more young nymphs. Frequent handling of egg-bearing females may cause them to abort their egg capsules, which in itself is not fatal to either female or eggs, but which may result in egg desiccation or feeding damage by other roaches.

Rearing Instructions

Any type of cage covered with ordinary window screen will work well for rearing these roaches. Even the smallest nymphs are too large to squeeze through the mesh. Some absorbent material, such as sand, sawdust or crushed corncob (available at pet stores), should be placed in the bottom of the cage. This material should be replaced every 4 to 6 months. Pour the used material through a sieve to avoid throwing away any small nymphs. These are tropical insects, so place the cage in a warm location. They seem to do best at about 80° F. Also, the roaches prefer subdued light, so don't keep them in an area with bright lights (don't use an incandescent light bulb to warm them; an infrared bulb, like those used to keep food warm, works much better).

Food. Fresh fruits or vegetables, such as lettuce, carrots, celery tops, apples, or potatoes are the primary diet. The vegetable diet should be supplemented with protein-rich foods such as powdered milk, meat scraps, fresh liver, or dry dog food. A high-protein dry dog food can be fed directly from the package, no pulverizing is necessary. Also, since apples and potatoes are high in moisture, at least for a while, they may eliminate the need for a separate supply of drinking water.

Water. A supply of drinking water is important for roach survival. If necessary, use a "drinking fountain" to provide water to the roaches.

Tracheal mites. These roaches are frequently infested with tiny yellowish or whitish tracheal mites. These mites live in the trachea of the roaches, but are frequently seen wandering about on the surface of the roaches' body. If these mites become overly abundant they may irritate your roaches, resulting in poor growth and vigor. While these mites will not harm humans, many people are nervous about seeing these tiny parasites on a cockroach that they may be handling at the time. Periodically inspecting the roaches and removing mites with a soft artist's brush can help reduce the problem. Some hissing roach cultures are certified as "mite-free", so you might want to obtain your livestock from one of these sources to avoid this problem.

PRAYING MANTIS
(Mantis and Stagmomantis spp.)

Background Information

Mantids appear awkward and as clumsy as an engineer's nightmare. They are equipped with six legs, like all other insects. The first two to help determine distance and grasp prey. The remaining four help walk, each independently operated, hold on to a slippery surface, or hang from a twig, while holding a squirming prey in the two front legs. The two antenna can, reportedly, determine if an approaching movement is by something warm blooded, friend or foe. Two compound eyes and a head that can turn 180 degrees in either direction make them especially observant.

If you don't have mantises in your area but would like to rear them, egg cases can be purchased by mail from garden and biological control supply companies (see "The Insect Study Sourcebook"). Mantis egg cases look as though they are made of a foamy, papermache material. The cases are a masterpiece of design, and can hold up to 100 little mantids, and can protect them from the winter elements.

Rearing Instructions

<u>Raising</u> <u>Mantids</u> <u>Outdoors</u>. When you receive your egg cases, they should be attached to shrubbery using a trash bag tie or a similar water resistant material. If you are located in an area where snow can be expected, be certain to install them on the shrubs above the expected snow line. In the event that you receive egg cases during warm weather and are unable to place them outdoors immediately, place them in a refrigerator to prevent them from hatching prematurely. Tiny newly hatched mantis can be difficult to raise to adulthood even under the best of circumstances, so you don't want them to hatch until you are prepared to supply them with food.

<u>Raising</u> <u>Mantids</u> <u>in</u> <u>Captivity</u>. If you wish to observe the hatching and life cycle of mantids, you might elect to let one or more egg cases hatch in captivity. The mantids will be born hungry, and so they will need a source of small insects (like aphids or fruit flies). If this type of food is not available when the egg cases arrive, place the nests in the refrigerator until you can secure an ample supply of small insects. Any type of suitable rearing container may be used. One easy method for observing the hatch is to use a large paper shopping bag. Cut a rectangular opening in one side of the bag and install a clear plastic window. Note that the top can be folded and held with paper clips after the egg case is placed inside. Make at least 25 tiny holes near the top of the bag for air circulation.

When you install the plastic picture window, cellophane tape is the most convenient way to attach the plastic to the bag, but make sure that the sticky side of the tape is not exposed in the area where the mantids will walk. Mantids have tiny, delicate feet and if any sticky area is exposed they might get stuck and it will be difficult to get them free with out causing damage to their feet. Also, do not place more than one egg case in a paper bag. Mantids are born hungry and will experiment with their killing skills even when they aren't hungry. Hatchlings from one egg case will cause problems when the second egg case hatches. Mantids from the first egg case will immediately start killing mantids from the other nest.

If you're really lucky, you might get to see some of the mantids emerge from the zipper area of the egg case still in their membrane sacks. Usually one end of the sack remains attached to the egg case so that the mantid, usually with its head out will be able to kick and squirm its way out of the sack. A close examination of a newly evacuated nest will show material on the sides of the zipper area that looks like saw dust; this is the shreds of the membrane sacks that each mantis had been in during the hatching process.

When they hatch, mantid nymphs are very small, less than 10mm in length. Usually mantids hatch from their egg cases in mid June or later.

Select a few of the largest and most vigorous mantids for rearing. The rest may be released outdoors. It is best to scatter the little mantids about the yard or garden, so that they can hunt for insects and are not tempted to eat each other. In the event that you have more than one nest to hatch, you may want to divide the area to avoid releasing tiny mantids where you may have released other mantids previously. In mid September adult mantids will generally be found in the same areas where they were released earlier in the year.

Housing one mantis per box is best, you will have an opportunity to select pairs for mating when you allow them to exercise indoors in an "exercise area". It is a good policy to clean each mantis cage at least once each week. While cleaning the cages one at a time, you can place the mantids on house plants (watch out for insecticides!) or on a "bouquet" of twigs or small branches from outdoor shrubs or trees as a place to climb and get exercise. When in captivity, many females make their egg cases in November. However, we have more females now making their egg cases in December and they are larger egg cases.

Mantids are general predators, and will consume all types of live insects. Without a source of other insects in the first 24 to 48 hours of life the mantids will begin to eat each other. Also, don't be alarmed if large numbers of the mantids die in the first week - this is common. You can feed them insects that you gather outdoors, or you can feed them flies, mealworms, or crickets from reared cultures (or the pet shop). In captivity, one cricket every other day seems to be the proper amount of food for mature mantids.

Water, applied daily as a mist to cotton balls or plant foliage, will serve as a source of water. Apparently mantids need very little water, as they usually obtain the necessary moisture they need from the insects they consume. The only exception to this is when they first emerge from their egg case. If the mantis nymphs do not get water within the first 12 hours of emerging, they will die. A small bottle or a test tube with a moist wick will do nicely.

INDIAN STICK INSECT
(Carausius morosus)

Background Information
This stick insect is native to India, but can be easily reared in the temperate regions. These stick insects feign death and assume a rigid, pencil-like attitude when touched between the middle and hind legs. They resume normal activity when "tickled" at the outer 1/3 of the abdomen.

Description. When fully grown, the Indian stick insect measures from four to five inches. The color is usually green/fawn and sometimes speckled, and in rare instances dark forms also occur. Everyone who has kept stick insects knows the wonderful camouflage given by its resemblance to a twig or leaf stem. It usually lies flat against the stalk of its foodplant, and unless you know what you're looking for, you may not be able to recognize it, even when kept in a small box. When alarmed, the insect feigns death and assumes a rigid posture, which gives a more stick-like appearance. A series of 6 molts are undergone during life, and at this time the insect refuses food. Unlike most insects they are able to regenerate lost legs, at least in part. These stick insects are active primarily at night.

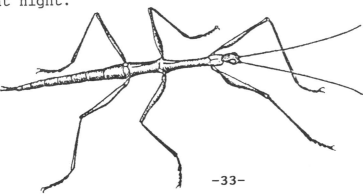

Eggs. The dark brown eggs are small, round and, seed-like. The adult female drops 4-9 eggs every night along with the frass. These eggs need to be separated from the frass and stored in containers. The eggs can take up to six months to hatch.

Nymphs. The young stick insects are very similar in appearance to the adults, except for being smaller. They molt 4 - 5 times before becoming mature adults.

Adults. The mature stick insects are usually green or dark brown in color. They are predominantly all females, with males being extremely rare (1 in 10,000 individuals). The males are generally more slender with proportionally longer antennae and larger legs than the females. Also, they have a red band on the underside of the thorax.

Rearing Instructions

Care and Food. Indian stick insect will feed on privet leaves (Ligustrum vulgare) in captivity, though ivy leaves (Hedera helix) can also be offered with success. If you feed them ivy, make sure to wash the soot, dust and other contaminants off the leaves. The foodplant should be kept in a jar of water, but be careful to plug the top with cotton to prevent insects from drowning. Change the food plant every other day, and when doing this, make sure there are no stick insects on the discarded stems - they are almost invisible. They can be handled if care is used, but a camel hair brush should be used for young ones.

Stick insects are "edge feeders", that is they nibble the leaves from the edge and not the surface. They are nocturnal in habits and usually feed in an irregular pattern, eating much one day and little the next. Food consumption doubles after each molt.

Water. After hatching, young stick insects are very thirsty and seek water to drink. Afterwards, however, they avoid water until their lives draw to a close. When dying, they are unable to eat, so can no longer absorb moisture through their food. At this time, they usually seek out water, and remain with their mouths immersed in it for some time.

Housing. They are best kept in a ventilated cage at normal room temperature. The cage must be at least 18" tall to allow for sufficient "headroom" during the molting process. Do not place by a window, and do not use artificial light, as they dislike bright light. While numbers of stick insects can be kept together, they cannot be kept with other insects.

Behavior. During the daytime they are sleepy and not easily aroused. They become active at night and cannibalism sometimes occurs. If you see an insect bite off the limb of another, this is usually an indication that they are not being properly fed, or they are overcrowded.

Breeding. Stick insects are parthenogenetic, that is to say that females can reproduce without fertilization by males. The male, however, does occasionally appear and can be distinguished by its longer antennae and slender build. When 9 months old the females begin to lay eggs. These are scattered on the floor of the cage and are easily mistaken for excreta material. Hatching takes from 4 to 10 months, but usually the insects hatch in the fifth month. The eggs need no special care, but very damp conditions must be avoided.

Diseases. The most common disease is caused by a fungus. They are more susceptible to diseases if overcrowded, or by neglecting to keep the cage clean. If the whole stock is diseased it is better to get rid of them and start again.

AUSTRALIAN STICK INSECT
(Extatosoma tiaratum)

Background Information

This magnificent stick insect comes from the jungle areas of Australia, where it feeds on Eucalyptus.

The mottled brown and black eggs are quite large (about 4 x 5 mm) and have a cream white band on each side. The eggs should be kept on moist sand (as with most stick insect eggs) during their six month incubation period.

Newly hatched nymphs are extremely active and quite large (about 2.5 cm long). They run around with their tails curled up. Their red heads, white "collars", and black bodies are, in fact, quite different from the adults' colors, whereas most stick insect nymphs resemble their parents.

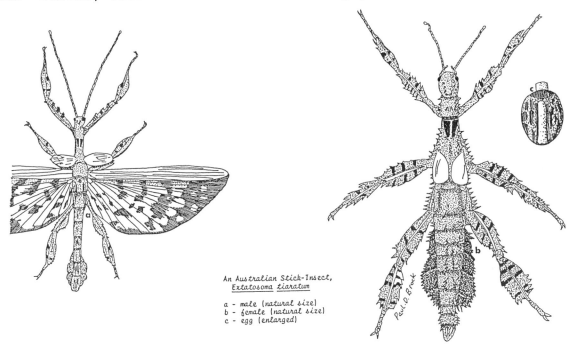

An Australian Stick-Insect,
Extatosoma tiaratum

a - male (natural size)
b - female (natural size)
c - egg (enlarged)

Rearing Instructions

Newly hatched tiaratum nymphs should be kept in tightly closed plastic boxes with foodplant leaves. They can be fed bramble (Rubus spp.) (blackberry or raspberry); they will also eat eucalyptus and oak. A temperature of at least 70°F is required. Nymphs should therefore be kept in either a warm room, or in a cage with a lightbulb to provide heat. The nymphs like humidity, which is not difficult to maintain in their plastic boxes. The food should be sprayed lightly with water every day (nymphs of all sticks appreciate this).

After about two days, the nymphs stop wandering inside the box and change color to brown; this is not a molt. Molting does occur seven or eight times during development, and the brown color is retained throughout their growth period. In successive instars, they become more spiky and leaf-like, with foliose expansions of the legs. Adulthood is attained after five or six months, and adults live a further six months or more. Sexing of nymphs is easy - the males are thinner and not so prickly as the females; their wings develop earlier and their tails are less exquisitely designed.

Adult males are about 13 cm long, brown, with huge mottled gray and white wings. Adult females are brown, very prickly, and quite heavy. They are usually 15 cm or more in length, with vestigial wings, much too small to fly with. With both sexes present, one has to have males and females in a cage to obtain pairings and fertile eggs, unlike species such as the Indian stick insects (Carausius morosus), which is parthenogenetic Of all stick insects in which both sexes are known, males are usually rare. In tiaratum, an exception, males are almost as common as females.

Since this insects grows throughout the year, a good source of the foodplant is required. Bramble is sometimes difficult to obtain in winter, but can be found in sheltered places. If the only bramble available has partly discolored leaves, the brown parts should be cut off, as they are too hard for the insects to chew. If you do not have a dependable source of bramble, you may want to gather acorns for growing during the winter months.)

BROWN STICK INSECT
(Anisomorpha buprestoides)

Background Information
This stick insect is native to the southern United States. They are a rather plump stick insect (especially the female), being light brown with bold black stripes along the back and sides. The robust legs are dark brown and the antennae are relatively short, at least for a stick insect.

The larger nymphs and adults give off an extremely powerful odor when disturbed. This is probably an adaptation to scare off predators. When the nymphs are small they have a habit of resting near each other; sometimes they will lie on top of one another.

Rearing Instructions
The egg is dark brown, and measures 3 mm long by 1.5 mm wide. The eggs should be kept on moist sand in a plastic box until they hatch. The nymphs should be placed in a plastic box with brambles as the foodplant. The leaves should be misted with water, for two purposes. The nymphs like to drink the water droplets, and it provided them with a humid atmosphere (which most stick insects need). They can be kept in a warm room with a temperature of about 70°F.

EASTERN SUBTERRANEAN TERMITE
(Reticulitermes flavipes)

Background Information

Most termites live in tropical and subtropical environments. They build nests in soil, earthen mounds or wood. Of the 41 species of termites that live in the United States, most of them occur in the southwest. The Eastern subterranean termite, Reticulitermes flavipes (Kollar), occurs throughout much of eastern temperate North America and has been assisted by our desire to construct wood buildings and other structures that provide termites with food, moisture and shelter.

At first glance subterranean termites resemble "white ants". A closer inspection reveals several prominent differences. The termites have a thorax which is broadly joined to the abdomen (ants have a constricted, "hourglass" waist); termite antennae are straight and composed of bead-like segments (ants have slender antennae which are "elbowed"); and, termite reproductives have two pairs of wings that are equally sized and lacking crossveins (ants have hind wings that are significantly smaller than the forewings). Termites are small (1/4 to 1/2 inch), softbodied, pale (dirty white) insects. Soldier termites have heavily armored, darkly pigmented heads and jaws and the reproductives, in contrast, are usually dark brown or black. Worker and soldier termites also generally lack eyes.

Biology and Life Cycle.

Termites develop through gradual metamorphosis, with 5 to 6 molts required for maturation. This process usually stops in the last nymphal stage and the individuals become workers. Those that complete the passage into adulthood, but do not become sexually mature, become either workers or soldiers.

After a brief mating flight in the spring of the year the fertile males (kings) and females (queens) shed their wings and establish a new colony in the soil. The eggs and nymphs are cared for and protected by special workers and soldiers. Though these sterile worker and soldier termites are of both sexes, their reproductive development is suppressed by hormones secreted by the king and queen. If the original king and queen die the lack of these hormones will permit more reproductives to develop very quickly. Also, colonies may produce supplemental reproductives at other times to "boost" a colonies reproduction, if conditions warrant. Female termites are known to lay millions of eggs each year and may live for up to 20 years (probably less than 10 years for the subterranean termites). Non-reproductive termites, on the other hand, usually live for only a couple of years. Individual termite colonies have been known to exist for up to 100 years!

The termites are closely related to the cockroaches, but like the ants, termites are also social insects. However, the evolutionary origin of termite social behavior is entirely different from that of ants, bees and wasps. Termites live in large colonies of cooperating individuals of three different castes. A caste is a group of insects that performs certain highly specialized tasks. The three termite castes are the reproductives, workers and soldiers. The termites castes, unlike those of the ants, are composed of both sexes (not just females). Termite reproductives are the elite and they are provided with every necessity of life by the soldiers and workers. The soldiers are sterilized adults that are specialized for defending the colony. They have large mandibles and heavily armored heads. The workers are the most populous caste, and they are responsible for building the nest and galleries, cleaning and maintaining the nest, collecting food and feeding the members of the soldier and reproductive castes.

The termites' greatest hazard is a harsh environment; they are very susceptible to desiccation and so they remain secluded in their damp, dark, climate-controlled nests, avoiding exposure to the air. They often build special additions onto their nests (in the form of mud tubes) in order to reach new sources of food. Ants are the major animal predators of termites. Sometimes entire termite colonies are wiped out by tiny parasitic nematodes (worms).

Termites are important "recyclers" of wood in nature. By tunneling through wood termites create entryways for moisture and decay fungi to speed the decomposition of wood into humus. Termites derive their nutrition from the cellulose that is contained in the wood. The digestion of the wood is accomplished by microbial bacteria and protozoans that reside in the intestinal tract of the termites. Young termites are "inoculated" with cultures of this bacteria and protozoans through feeding by the worker termites. In fact, it has been shown that if these microoriganisms are artificially removed from the termite gut, the termite will starve to death even though it continues to feed on wood.

The Eastern subterranean termite normally lives in nests located in the soil, traveling out to nearby sources of cellulose (trees, logs, stumps, woodpiles, fenceposts, lumber, paper, and cardboard) to feed. The termites remain hidden within the moist, protective confines of the soil and wood. If they must travel across stone, masonry or concrete surfaces they construct special mud tubes.

Rearing Instructions

Small colonies of eastern subterranean termites can be easily maintained in one gallon glass jars. Termite colonies can often be found outdoors under logs, woodpiles, and in old stumps. If at all possible, when gathering live termites try to include reproductives (darker body and/or winged individuals) or a queen along with the workers and soldiers. However, even colonies composed entirely or workers and soldiers will last for at least several months.

Fill the bottom of the jar with 4 to 6 inches of slightly moistened soil (preferably from the same area as the termite colony). Place a block of wood (softwood lumber works great) on the surface of the soil and add the live termites to the jar. The termites will begin constructing tunnels in the soil and the wood. If you keep the jar in a dark location they will generally tunnel along side of the glass, as well as in the interior of the soil mass. The wood block will provide the necessary food. Occasionally remoistening the soil is the only other necessary maintenance.

EUROPEAN EARWIG
(Forficula auricularia)

Background Information
Earwigs are primarily a tropical and subtropical group of insects, and there are only 28 species of earwigs in the United States, and at least several of these are introduced from other continents. The name earwig is derived from the ancient belief that these insects would crawl into the ears of sleeping people and bore into the inner ear and brain causing insanity. There is, of course, no truth to this legend!

Biology and Life Cycle.
Earwigs are elongate, flattened and somewhat roach-like in appearance, but they can be immediately identified by the pincer-like appendages at 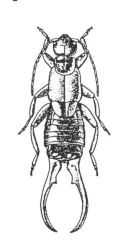 the tip of the abdomen. These cerci are used for defense, prey capture, mating and wing unfolding. The forewings of most earwigs are short and leathery in texture. The membranous hindwings, which are much larger, are completely hidden beneath the forewings. Despite the large hindwings and the ability to fly, earwigs prefer to escape danger by running (usually with the pincer-like cerci arched over their back). One common earwig in United States is the common European earwig (Forficula auricularia). The European earwig was not known to occur in the United States prior to 1900. They are a native of Europe, western Asia, and north Africa and were first reported from the Pacific Northwest and southern New England shortly after the turn of the century. This earwig is generally about 1/2 inch long, reddish-brown, dark brown or black in color, and with slender antennae are only reach 1/2 as long as the body. The immatures (nymphs) resemble the adults in appearance, except for their smaller size, grayish-brown color and lack of wings.

Earwigs pass through three stages of development (gradual metamorphosis) and the rate of development is dependent on the temperature (20 to 70 days). The male and female earwigs spend the winter as pairs or small groups in protected quarters, often in underground burrows. In the spring the female evicts the male and egg-laying begins. The female watches over her 20 to 50 small, white eggs, chasing away all intruders including the male. She also protects them from desiccation and mold by licking them repeatedly. Even after the nymphs hatch from the eggs the female will continue to care for her brood. As the nymphs approach maturity they gain independence from their mother and by late summer and early fall they are fully grown. In the temperate regions there are generally two generations each year.

Earwigs are predominantly nocturnal scavengers, feeding on soft vegetative matter like decaying foliage, algae, fungi, sprouts and seedlings, flower petals, pollen and corn silks, but they are also known to feed on other insects and small invertebrates (dead or alive). When hunting live prey they sometimes use their cerci to grasp the prey and pass it over their back to the mouth. The plant material almost always constitutes the bulk of their diet. When the sun comes up the earwigs gather in groups beneath stones, logs, boards and other objects on the ground.

Rearing Instructions

To obtain adult earwigs, all one has to do is search under debris, logs and stones near houses and other buildings. Once a suitable spot is found and earwigs are located, put them in a jar with your fingers (don't worry about the abdominal pincers (cerci), as they can't administer more than a small pinch). They may also be easily gathered by using pitfall traps (without preservative, of course).

Once you get your captives home, you can start thinking about preparing a place for them. An ordinary glass-walled aquarium is a perfect container, and any size from one gallon up will do nicely.

The first step in preparing the aquarium is to fill it with a 1/2 inch of layer of gravel followed by a 1 to 2 inch layer of soil. It should be deeper at one end of the container than the other. A flat rock and/or piece of wood/board should be placed in the container and some small plants may be added to the terrarium, if desired. The lower end should be kept constantly moist by misting it as needed. A piece of glass, plastic or netting makes a good lid, and prevents the earwigs from crawling out.

Food. Since earwigs are scavengers, feeding them is usually no problem. They will eat almost anything they can sink their mandibles into. Flies, worms, crickets, or any other small creatures make fine live food. In the winter they can be fed mealworms or other insects that can be reared as food. They can also be fed bits of meat (cooked chicken or raw hamburger), dogfood, soft plant materials (especially bits of pulpy fruit), or possibly even dead insects.

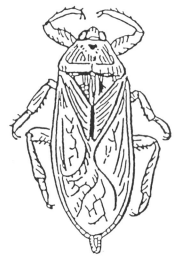

GIANT WATER BUGS
(Lethocerus and Belostoma spp.)

Rearing Instructions

These large insects can be kept in any good aquarium. Lethocerus is not fussy about its water conditions. However, it does appreciate having some water plants and /or stones in its tank. The techniques outlined under "Rearing Aquatic Insects" on page 20 also apply to rearing giant water bugs.

They can be fed many types of fish (goldfish, guppie, kuhlii loach, banjo catfish, etc.) and insects (crickets, mealworms, predaceous diving beetles, etc.). Three of these fish possess poisonous spines, but this does not hinder the giant water bug! The size of its food doesn't discourage them either, as they will take fish up to 3 inches long.

OTHER WATER BUGS
(Corixidae, Notonectidae, Nepidae and Gerridae)

Rearing Instructions

Other water bugs, especially water boatmen (Corixidae), backswimmers (Notonectidae), waterscorpions (Nepidae) and water striders (Gerridae), can also be maintained in an aquarium. The water boatmen feed upon minute detritus, whereas the backswimmers and waterscorpions are predators feeding on small aquatic organisms. The water striders are scavengers and feed upon dead or struggling insects on the water's surface. The techniques outlined under "Rearing Aquatic Insects" on page 20 will get you started with rearing these insects.

LARGE MILKWEED BUG
(Oncopeltus fasciatus)

Background Information
The large milkweed bug is ideal for rearing projects. It is brightly colored and easy to maintain. It requires little space, is easily observed, creates no offensive odor, is resistant to diseases and parasites, and has a fairly short life cycle. This species is widely distributed throughout the United States and can be readily collected during the proper season.

Collecting milkweed bugs. Milkweed bugs are collected from their host plants, milkweeds (Asclepias species), which commonly grow in pastures and along roadsides. The plants are 3 to 5 feet tall with stems and large, fleshy leaves that contain a milky juice, or latex. The seeds are borne in pods. As the pods "ripen" they turn brown and split open, releasing the seeds (each bearing a silky tuft of down). In most areas the pods appear toward the end of summer; therefore, late summer and early fall are the best times to search for milkweed bugs. The bugs begin to appear on the milkweed plants as the pods mature. The larger milkweed bug does not overwinter in northern states and must reinvade the state each year from areas to the south. Adults and older nymphs will be found feeding on milkweed pods and the seeds they contain. You will find more bugs on pods which have begun to split open. The bugs are easy to see because of their bright reddish-orange and black markings, and they are easy to collect by hand. Collect both adults and nymphs, and place them in your collecting container. You will also need to collect a lot of milkweed pods to feed your bugs over the next year.

Purchasing milkweed bugs. Special strains of large milkweed bugs that are able to survive on unsalted sunflower kernels are now available through biological supply houses. The advantage of buying these bugs is that you don't have to collect milkweed seed to use as food.

Biology and Life Cycle
Eggs. The oval, yellowish eggs are laid in clusters of 10 to 50. The newly-laid eggs look very much like miniature jellybeans. The eggs hatch within 1 to 2 weeks when held at 70 to 80° F. They change from yellow to reddish-orange during incubation.

Nymphs. Newly-emerged nymphs are bright red and about the size of a pinhead. They crawl about actively looking for food almost immediately after hatching. The nymphs grow fairly quickly through their five nymphal stages (instars). Wingpads appear early in development.

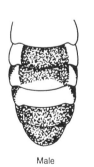 

Male   Female

Adults. Milkweed bugs reach adulthood after the fifth nymphal molt. Fully developed wings are characteristic of the adult stage. The male and female can be distinguished by examining the ventral abdominal surface. In the male, the second abdominal segment (counting from the thorax) is unspotted, the third segment bears a wide black band and the fourth segment has a somewhat narrow black band. The female's second abdominal segment has two black spots, the third segment has a wide black band and the fourth has two black spots (not a narrow band like the male).

Large milkweed bugs mate in an end-to-end position. They couple at any hour of the day or night, and mating pairs may remain attached for 30 minutes or more. If the colony is kept at about 80° F. the eggs will develop to adulthood in about 25 to 30 days.

Rearing Instructions

Rearing container. The large milkweed bug adapts well to rearing in glass or plastic containers. Fish bowls or gallon jars covered with screening or cheesecloth are quite suitable.

The bugs are fully capable of flying, but in captivity they seem to prefer crawling around the container, but will readily climb the vertical glass or plastic walls. It's good idea to ring the mouth of the container with a thin layer of mineral oil, petroleum jelly or furniture wax. This will keep the bugs from escaping when the cover is removed for house-keeping, etc. The bottom of the container should be lined with material for the bugs to crawl on; paper towels cut to the same dimensions as the container will work well. Keep the cage clean and avoid overcrowding.

Food. Milkweed bugs require milkweed seeds for proper growth and development (unless you're using the sunflower seed strain). Milkweed seeds are not available commercially, so you'll have to collect your own supply. This is easily done when you collect your bugs. Pods which have recently split open are just right for collecting, but you can take green pods as well. After the pods are dry, separate the seeds from the pod and down. The dry seeds can be stored indefinitely at room temperature. Generation after generation of milkweed bugs will develop on a diet of seeds (milkweed or sunflower) and water. Used seeds should be discarded periodically.

Water. Milkweed bugs need a water source. The most convenient way to water them is with a "vial and wick" fountain. Soiled wicks should be replaced frequently.

Egg Laying Sites. Small balls of cheesecloth are suitable sites for egg-laying (oviposition). They can be easily removed and transferred to other containers for starting new colonies. The eggs will hatch right in the cheesecloth and the young nymphs will crawl out.

STINK BUGS
(Euschistus and Achrosternum spp.)

Background Information
The plant feeding members of the stink bug family (Pentatomidae) are easily reared. They require little space, are easily observed, and only produce their offensive odor when disturbed or handled. The predatory species are more difficult to rear, requiring live prey for food, and so instructions for only the plant feeding species are given here. Species such as the dusky stink bug (Euschistus tristigmus), the one-spotted stink bug (E. variolarius), the brown stink bug (E. servus), and the green stink bug (Achrosternum hilare) are widely distributed and can be readily collected during the warm season. They can be found feeding an a variety of plants and are common pests on many agricultural crops. Collect both adults and nymphs, and place them in your collecting container.

Biology and Life Cycle

Eggs. The oval eggs are laid in clusters of 10 to 50. The newly-laid eggs look very much like miniature barrels. The eggs hatch within 1 to 2 weeks when held at 70 to 80° F.

Nymphs. Newly-emerged nymphs are much smaller than the adults. They crawl about actively looking for food almost immediately after hatching. The nymphs grow fairly quickly through their five nymphal stages (instars). Wingpads appear early in development.

Adults. Stink bugs reach adulthood after the fifth nymphal molt. Fully developed wings are characteristic of the adult stage. The adult stink bugs mate in an end-to-end position. They couple at any hour of the day or night, and mating pairs may remain attached for 30 minutes or more. If the colony is kept at about 80° F the eggs will develop to adulthood in about 25 to 30 days.

Rearing Instructions

Rearing container. Stink bugs adapt well to rearing in glass or plastic containers. Fish bowls or gallon jars covered with screening or cheesecloth are quite suitable.

The bugs are fully capable of flying, but in captivity they seem to prefer crawling around the container, but will readily climb the vertical glass or plastic walls. It's good idea to ring the mouth of the container with a thin layer of mineral oil, petroleum jelly or furniture wax. This will keep the bugs from escaping when the cover is removed for house-keeping, etc. The bottom of the container should be lined with material for the bugs to crawl on; paper towels cut to the same dimensions as the container will work well. Keep the cage clean and avoid overcrowding. With a relative humidity of less than 50% and a temperature of around 75°F, the rearing containers seldom require attention more than twice a week. If the humidity is high, the jars will "sweat" and fungus diseases can break out unexpectedly. If a disease outbreak occurs, discard any infected individuals and sterilize the jars with scalding water before reusing them.

Food. Stink bugs require fresh plant foods for proper growth and development. The easiest and most successful food material are green snap beans. The beans are available throughout the year at most grocery stores, and a pound of beans will feed up to 200 adult stink bugs for a week. Make sure you thoroughly wash the beans to remove any pesticide residues before feeding them to your stink bugs. Keep the extra beans in the refrigerator.

Egg Laying Sites. Small balls of cheesecloth are suitable sites for egg-laying (oviposition). They can be easily removed and transferred to other containers for starting new colonies. The eggs will hatch right in the cheesecloth and the young nymphs will crawl out.

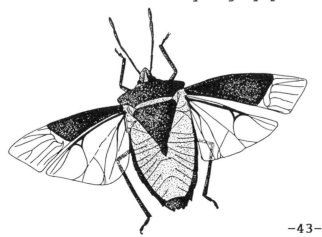

ANTLIONS
(Hesperoleon spp.)

Background Information

The antlion is a very interesting insect. The larvae feed on ants and other small insects. To capture prey, with as little effort as possible, the antlions construct an ingenious ant trap: a funnel shaped pit made in loose soil or light sand. With remarkable engineering skill, the pit's walls are pitched at an angle that makes them just of the verge of stability.

The antlion larva, armed with a formidable pair of mandibles, buries itself in the pit's bottom. In time, an ant or other small insect passes too closely to the pit's steep sides. A small avalanche invariably follows, delivering the hapless prey to the antlion's jaws. Sometimes the larva will assist the prey's demise by throwing bits of sand at it with its mandibles.

Because of their unique lifestyle, antlions are limited in their choice of environments and must live where there is loose, dry sand. In regions such as the American southwest this is no problem, but in less sandy regions they can be found in sandy areas which are protected from heavy rains. Sometimes dozens of pits can be found clustered together under a rocky ledge or cave entrance. Sometimes they can be found on the sandy shoulders of dirt roads and trails.

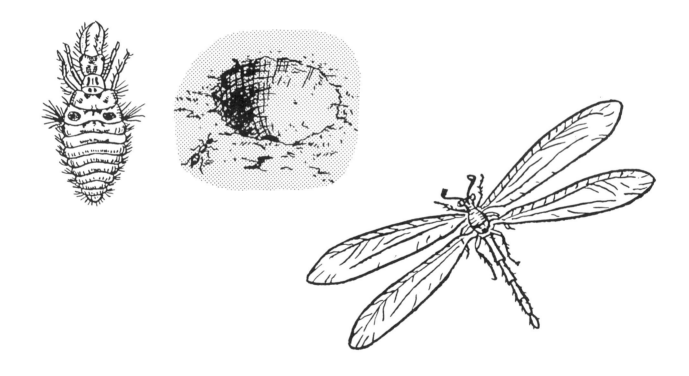

Antlions undergo complete metamorphosis. The pupa is formed in a spherical cocoon made of sand. When the adult emerges it resembles a damselfly with short, clubbed antennae. Occasionally they fly to lights in the summer. Some sources say that the adults do not feed; others report that they feed on flying insects. They are weak flyers, however, and any but the slowest insects would have no trouble eluding them.

Rearing Instructions

Larvae can be collected with a small trowel or spoon. A simple procedure is to dig up a funnel and pour the sand through a small screen (a butterfly net will also work). Live larvae should be kept in separate vials. They are not known to be cannibalistic, but it is always a good idea to play it safe with carnivorous species. A word of restraint is called for here. In the wooded northeastern states at least, antlion habitats are few and far between. It is suggested that you limit the number of larvae you take, especially if the population is small.

Larvae can be kept in a shallow container, such as a plastic sweater box. This should be filled with about an inch of dry sand. Several larvae can be introduced, depending on the size of the cage. A screen or netting lid is required to prevent prey insects from escaping. In captivity, antlions can be fed with ants, aphids, small mealworms, and many other similar small insects. Live food is essential. (Antlion larvae may be able to survive long periods of time with no food whatsoever. This is probably an important adaptation to their lifestyle, since they may wait a long time for prey to fall in their trap.) The sand should be lightly misted with water about twice a week. Antlions do not seem to need much moisture. Indeed, if it becomes damp enough that the sand grains cling together, the results may be fatal.

TIGER BEETLES
(Cicindelidae)

Background Information

The tiger beetles make exceptionally interesting subjects for study in captivity. Most North American tiger beetles belong to the genus Cicindela, although there are three other genera, the members of which are nocturnal. Cicindela are active, often attractive, and easily kept if simple precautions are observed. A tank full of tiger beetles can provide hours of fascinating observation, as tiger beetles, unlike other beetles, are always "on the go". Their actions are always interesting, and sometimes even comical. Keeping an accurate note book on the habits of your "tigers" makes keeping them even more enjoyable, and your records will have scientific value.

To obtain adult tiger beetles, all one has to do is find an open, bare area (sand, gravel, clay or alkali soils are often productive), and walk about on it watching for beetles to fly up about 2 to 3 meters ahead. Once a beetle is located, sneak up on it with a net (it is almost impossible to catch one without one), and quickly place it over the beetle. Then it can be removed with the fingers, and placed in a bottle of some sort. Some people might be alarmed by the dangerous-looking mandibles, but even the largest of them can do more than give a slight pinch.

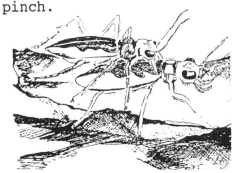

Mating tiger beetles.

Tiger beetle larva in burrow.

Female cicindelid ovipositing.

Rearing Instructions

Once you get your captives home, you can start thinking about preparing a place for them. An ordinary glass-walled aquarium is a perfect container, and any size from one gallon up will do nicely.

The first step in preparing the aquarium is to fill it with about 1 inch of soil or sand, preferably of the same type on which the beetles were found. It should be deeper in one corner so they can dig burrows at night. A flat rock may be placed in this corner as they may prefer to burrow under that. Another corner should be kept constantly moist by pouring a small amount of water on it every day or so. Tiger beetles obtain moisture from wet ground, on which they "chew" to get water out of it. Failure to keep a watered area will cause the beetles to die of desiccation. This can happen very quickly - one or two days without water can kill most Cicindela. There should be no plants in the terrarium, as they will be uprooted and trampled, and serve no purpose. A piece of glass, plastic or netting makes a good lid, which prevents the beetles from flying out. Above the entire setup there should be a light source. A 60 watt light bulb provides both light and heat.

Food. Tiger beetles are voracious carnivores, and feeding them is usually no problem. They will eat almost anything they can sink their mandibles into. Flies, worms, crickets, or any other small creatures make fine tiger beetle food. In the winter they can be fed mealworms or other insects that can be reared as food. They will also, if given the chance, eat other tiger beetles, but this is rare if the beetles are all of the same size and well fed.

GROUND BEETLES
(Carabidae)

Background Information

The ground beetles are closely allied to the tiger beetles and may also be raised in captivity. There are hundreds of species in North America and at least two dozen species are common and widespread. Some of the larger ground beetles are quite active, sometimes attractive, and easily kept if simple precautions are observed.

To obtain adult ground beetles, all one has to do is search under debris, logs and stones in all types of habitats (especially forests, grasslands, and stream sides). Once a suitable spot is found and beetles are located, put them in a jar with your fingers (a net is seldom needed). They may also be easily gathered by using pitfall traps (without preservative, of course).

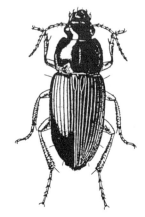

Rearing Instructions

Once you get your captives home, you can start thinking about preparing a place for them. An ordinary glass-walled aquarium is a perfect container, and any size from one gallon up will do nicely.

The first step in preparing the aquarium is to fill it with a 1/2 inch of layer of gravel followed by a 1 to 2 inch layer of soil (preferably of the same type on which the beetles were found. It should be deeper at one end of the container than the other. A flat rock and/or pieces of wood/board should be placed in the container and some small plants may be added to the terrarium, if desired. The lower end should be kept constantly moist by pouring a small amount of water on it every day. A piece of glass, plastic or netting makes a good lid, which prevents the beetles from flying or crawling out.

<u>Food</u>. Some ground beetles are voracious carnivores, and feeding them is usually no problem. They will eat almost anything they can sink their mandibles into. Flies, worms, crickets, or any other small creatures make fine ground beetle food. In the winter they can be fed mealworms or other insects that can be reared as food. Other ground beetles are scavengers feeding on bits of meat (cooked chicken or raw hamburger), soft plant materials (especially bits of pulpy fruit), or dead insects. Yet other ground beetles are seed eaters, and may do well on grass seed, birdseed (the millet seed, not sunflower seeds), or other plant seed gathered from outdoors.

CARRION BEETLE
(<u>Nicrophorus</u> <u>orbicollis</u>)

Background Information

Of all the beetles, perhaps the most interesting of all is the native species of burying beetle, <u>Nicrophorus</u> <u>orbicollis</u>. In the wild, <u>N.</u> <u>orbicollis</u> ranges from Hudson Bay to Florida and all the way to eastern Oklahoma, Kansas, Nebraska, and the Dakotas.

One very interesting physical characteristic of <u>N</u>. <u>orbicollis</u> is that they can both be sexed by looking at the markings above their mandibles. The females have an orange triangular shape, and the males have an orange square or rectangular marking.

Initially you can obtain beetles to rear by setting pitfall traps in May and June baited with fish and beefheart. The beetles should be raised in plastic containers, at least measuring 4" deep, 7" long, and 5" wide. The containers should be kept in a room which is at least 70°F.

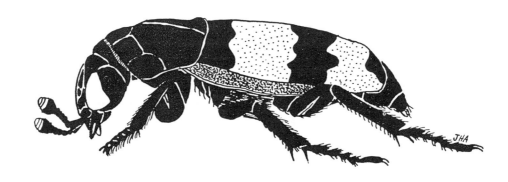

Rearing Instructions

In captivity, use mouse carcasses for N. orbicollis to bury and raise their broods on. The mice, which range from 15 to 30 grams, are keep frozen until needed, and then thawed at 70°F for 24 hours before being introducing the pair of beetles. In N. orbicollis, the carrion is usually buried within 24 hours. The female and male both participate in burial, and shaving the carcass of its fur. Then the beetles work the carcass into a "meatball" shape. The eggs are laid in a chamber near the carcass. When the larvae hatch they wander to the "meatball" where their parents await their arrival. Larval development is rapid with the eggs hatching in 2 days, being 1st larval instars for 1 day, second instar for 1 to 2 days, and finally third instar for 5 to 7 days. It is critical that one of the parent beetles be present during larval development. It is during this period that the parents feed the begging larvae regurgitated food from the carcass. A great deal of parental care occurs in the genus Nicrophorus. This is very rare among the coleopterans.

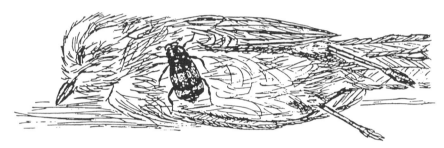

After 10 to 12 days, dig up the larvae and remove the male, if he has not already surfaced from the soil. The larvae and female are then put back in the soil in a "pseudochamber" that we make with our fist, along with whatever is left of the carcass. The female and carrion remains will be removed later, after the larvae have wandered and the female has surfaced to the top of the soil. In a few days the larvae begin to wander from the carcass and pupate.

The new beetles begin to emerge 40 to 45 days later. They are black and orange, active and have voracious appetites. For the first three weeks of their lives they should devour mealworms at an incredible rate. Later, they slow down to about two mealworms a day per beetle.

The size of the brood depends on the size of the carcass presented and upon how many larvae the parents cull.

MEALWORMS
(Tenebrio spp.)

Background Information

Mealworm larvae are excellent fish bait and can be used either alive or preserved. The yellow mealworm, Tenebrio molitor, is the species most frequently reared and used for bait. These beetle larvae are also used as food for exotic pets, such as lizards and tarantulas, and therefore can often be purchased in pet shops. They are also sold by bait dealers and biological supply companies.

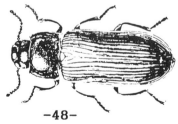

Yellow mealworm

Biology and Life Cycle

Larval mealworms molt 9 to 20 times during their development. If your mealworms are well-fed, warm (about 80° F), uncrowded, and exposed to sufficiently humid conditions, they will complete their development in about 5 months. On the average, the adults live for 84 days. Each female lays about 275 eggs.

Rearing Instructions

Any large glass or plastic container will work for rearing mealworms. Your mealworms will live well in a mixture of either graham flour and meat scraps or wheat bran with a small amount of dry brewer's yeast. Wheat bran alone seems to be an inadequate staple diet; the larvae will grow larger if you add yeast. You may also add oatmeal or poultry mash to the food medium if you like. Place 3 to 6 inches of food in the container. Add new food material every 4 to 6 months. Do not throw out the old media as it contains eggs and small larvae. Periodically you may need to sift out the excess amounts of old media, saving any mealworms and uneaten food.

Maintaining an adequate moisture supply is essential for mealworm survival; too little or too much moisture is equally bad. If there is too little moisture available, the larvae will grow slowly and will be small. If there is too much moisture, the food becomes moldy and poisons the larvae. To maintain suitable moisture levels place either a piece of cabbage, carrot or potato on top of the food. Replace it as needed (when it gets all dried out!). A separate supply of drinking water is not necessary, as the larvae are able to form water from the carbohydrates they consume.

When the larvae are nearly full-grown (about 3/4 to 1 inch long), place a piece of corrugated paper, crumpled paper towels, shredded paper, or burlap cloth in the container. Let the adult beetles emerge from these hiding places before disturbing them. Don't keep too many adults in one container. Crowding will eventually reduce the population, because the adults may begin to eat the eggs. Remove some of the adults when the colony has more than two or three adults per square inch. You can use these surplus adults to begin additional colonies, if you wish.

FLOUR BEETLES
(Tribolium confusum and Tribolium castaneum)

Background Information

Confused flour beetle

Two species of flour beetles commonly infest stored food products. They are the confused flour beetle (Tribolium confusum) and the red flour beetle (Tribolium castaneum). The species are very similar in size and appearance, but they can be easily distinguished by the difference in their antennae. The red flour beetle has an abrupt, distinctly three-segmented antennal club, whereas the confused flour beetle has a gradually swollen antennal club.

Biology and Life Cycle

Flour beetle eggs are very small (several would fit on the head of a pin). The whitish larvae are very active and burrow in the food medium. They pass through 6 to 11 instars, depending on the quality of their food and the temperature. You can determine the sex of the beetles as soon as they reach the pupal stage, but because they are so small you will need to use a low power microscope or a high power hand lens to do so. Examine the underside of the terminal abdominal segment. The females have a pair of small appendages. These males either have much smaller appendages or none at all.

Flour beetles average 3.4 mm in length. Although adults may live for up to 2 years, their average lifespan is only 6 months. The time it takes them required to complete development, from oviposition to adult emergence, varies with the environmental conditions. At 80° F and 75% relative humidity, the process takes about 40 days.

Rearing Instructions
Any medium to large size glass or plastic container is suitable for rearing flour beetles. Fill the container with an inch or two of white flour, finely-ground whole wheat flour or cornmeal. No water source is needed, but a piece of lettuce or potato will help maintain proper humidity.

Avoid overcrowding your cultures (which can lead to cannibalism or parasitism). Periodically transfer some beetles to a fresh food medium. The beetles should be transferred with some care because they are fairly delicate. Avoid using an aspirator to transfer the beetles, because they emit a disagreeable odor when disturbed. A small brush, spoon or spatula works better.

LADYBIRD BEETLES
(Coccinellidae)

Background Information
The ladybird beetles, commonly referred to as ladybugs, are highly beneficial insects because of their predatory habits. Both the adults and larvae feed on aphids, scale insects, mealybugs, and other small insects. Only one species, the Mexican bean beetle, feeds on plants and is considered a pest. The adult beetles vary in size from 3 to 8mm and they are broadly oval (almost spherical in some species) with a strongly convex upper surface. They are usually brightly colored in orange (or red, pink, or yellow) and black. The larvae are elongate and flattened and resemble tiny alligators.

Convergent lady beetle

Rearing Instructions
You can obtain live ladybugs from garden centers and biological control companies, or you can collect them in the wild. Since ladybird beetles are predatory you will have to keep them supplied with live aphids, whiteflies, mealybugs, or scale insects as food. There are at least two ways to accomplish this. First, you may rear larval and adult ladybugs in small plastic containers, providing them with live food by periodically introducing small amounts of plant foliage that has an aphid, mealybug, whitefly or scale colony on it. A sprouted potato, for example, can be conveniently infested with aphids. Or, you can place live potted plants with colonies of potential prey insects inside screen cages or other large containers. An occasional misting with water will provide droplets for drinking.

GRAIN AND BEAN WEEVILS
(Curculionidae and Bruchidae)

Background Information

Several types of weevils that are occasional stored food pests, including the rice, granary, maize and bean/pea weevils, can be reared in whole grain foods such as nuts, beans, cereals, fruits and seeds. Cultures can be started with adult weevils obtained from infested food products.

The rice weevil, granary weevil and maize weevils are true weevils (Curculionidae) and have a long snout on the head. The rice weevil

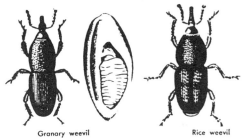

Granary weevil   Rice weevil

(Sitophilus oryzae) is about 3 mm long, dark reddish brown, with four pale spots on the upper surface. The rice weevil can fly and is attracted to lights. The granary weevil (Sitophilus granarius) is slightly larger (4 mm), of the same body shape and entirely dark chestnut-brown. It cannot fly and is not attracted to lights. The maize weevil (Sitophilus zeamaise) is also slightly larger than the rice weevil, and it is very dark reddish-brown or black with four yellowish spots. All of these weevils infest whole grain rice, barley, corn, wheat, popcorn, sunflower seeds, nuts, beans and bird seed. They will also attack hard cereal products such as macaroni, dry pet food, cereals, and caked flour.

The larvae are white, legless, and feed inside of the whole kernel or seed - hence they are rarely seen. Weevil damaged grains typically are hollow and have small, round emergence holes. The life cycle requires about 4 weeks and there may be three to five generations per year.

The bean weevils are not true weevils; they are members of the closely related bean weevil family (Bruchidae). Their body shape is more round than the rice, granary and maize weevils and they do not have the slender protruding snout of these true weevils. The common bean weevil is about 1/8 inch (3 mm) long with the upper surface mottled shades of gray. These feed on dried beans, leaving perfectly round holes in the beans.

Very often, beans are harvested from the garden which look perfectly good. However, there can be been weevil larvae present inside. These larvae can continue to develop while the beans are in storage, with adults emerging during winter.

Rearing Instructions

Any medium to large size glass or plastic container is suitable for rearing grain and bean weevils. Fill the container with an inch or two of whole grain rice, barley, corn, wheat, popcorn, sunflower seeds, nuts, and/or bird seed (for grain weevils), or dried beans or peas (for bean weevils).

Avoid overcrowding your cultures. Periodically transfer some beetles to a fresh food medium. A separate supply of water is generally not necessary.

Bean weevil

BUTTERFLIES AND MOTHS

General Rearing Procedures

You can start a moth or butterfly rearing program at any stage in the life cycle of these insects. Eggs and pupae (cocoons) can be purchased from biological supply companies or Lepidoptera breeders. Eggs and larvae can be collected in the field if you know where to look. To do this you must first learn what the common butterflies and moths are in your area and find out what their preferred larval food plants are. The female butterfly uses these plants for egg laying and if you check enough of these plants you are likely to find butterfly eggs. For example, if you would like to acquire a supply of black swallowtail (Papilio polyxenes) eggs, plant some parsley in your yard or garden.

The Process in a "Nutshell". Also, females can be used to attract and capture males and then you can breed your own butterflies or moths. After a male and female have mated, place the female (distinguished by their larger body size and narrower antennae) in a paper bag for oviposition. Some species will glue their eggs to the inside of the bag, and others will drop them to the bag's bottom (they may look like a sprinkling of sugar in the sack). After the eggs are laid, remove them from the bag and place groups of 20 eggs into separate hatching containers. If the eggs are glued to the sack, cut the sack around them and place the paper discs in the hatching containers. Any half-gallon or larger container will do.

Care of Female Butterflies

Very little attention has been given to the methods for obtaining eggs from female butterflies (and moths). The following techniques have been perfected over many years, and will prove successful for just about any species you might want to rear.

The Oviposition Cage. You will need to set up an ovipostion cage and related accessories. Most any available cage will work as an oviposition cage, but certain types have definite advantages over others. A soft cage made of netting is preferable to a hard wire cage, because the female will not damage her wings as quickly on the soft netting. Cylindrical cages seem better than square or rectangular ones because the female can fly around more naturally in it and there are no corners to trap her, which also helps to lessen wing damage. The preferred netting is ultrafine (no-see-um) mosquito netting. Since many females will lay some of their ova directly on the netting, use of ultrafine will keep all ova and hatching larvae inside, even tiny lycaenid larvae cannot escape through it. Two cage sizes will accommodate any butterfly. A small cylinder, 6 inches in diameter and 9 inches in height, will handle Lycaenidae, Hesperiidae, and others up to the size of Colias. A larger cylinder, 11 inches in diameter and 11 inches in height, will handle all larger species such as swallowtails and fritillaries.

The Light and Reflectors. While it is possible to obtain ova by placing a caged female outdoors in the sun, or on an outdoor shaded porch, or indoor on a sunny window, results will probably be erratic because control over such critical things as temperature, light intensity and humidity are limited. Chances are you will find the female dead from heat-stroke or desiccation before she has had a chance to lay her ova. It is better to use an indoor setup with lights and reflectors. A 75 to 100 watt incandescent light bulb in a fixture fitted with a 10 inch aluminum reflector will provide all the necessary

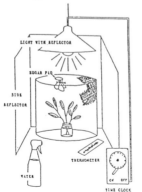

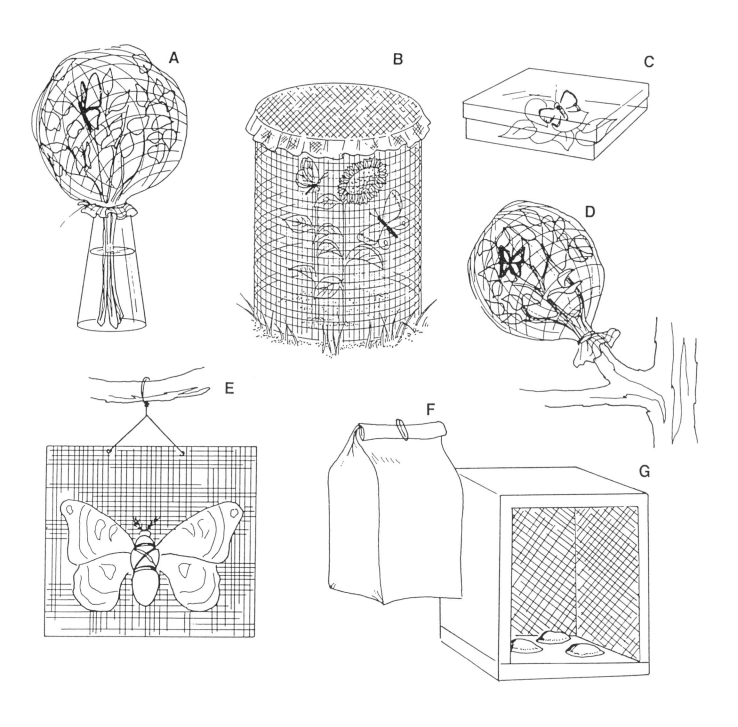

Techniques for rearing Lepidoptera: (a) bouquet of foliage set in a bottle of water and covered with nylon netting; (B) screen cage with plant growing inside; (C) plastic box with leaves; (D) nylon sack tied over a branch; (E) female moth tied to a screen to attract males; (F) paper sack for use as an egg laying (oviposition) chamber; and (G) emergence cage.

light and heat. The fixture should be suspended 6 to 12 inches above the top of the cage. Also, surround the cage with side reflectors to help increase the light intensity and hold heat from the light. You should have enough of these available to completely surround the cage or cages, since several cages fit under one light. These side reflectors can be made from a variety of materials, including aluminum sheeting, sheet metal, corrugated cardboard covered with aluminum foil, or reflectors for sunbathing.

The Thermometer. This is a necessary item. It is best kept on the table beside the bottom of the cage or cages. It can also be used on top of the cage to periodically check the temperature here. Try to maintain a temperature of 80° to 85°F at the bottom of the cage. The optimum temperature range that you want to maintain for the butterfly in the cage is 80° to 100°F. Do not let the temperature at the bottom of the cage exceed 100°F or the female will quickly die! The temperature should be regulated by raising or lowering the overhead light fixture, or by opening or closing the side reflectors.

Time Clocks. While not absolutely necessary for success, it is extremely helpful to have the lights regulated by an automatic time clock. The time settings are not critical and can be varied to fit your schedule. Generally speaking, they should be set to activate the lights from 8:00 AM to anywhere from 4:00 to 7:00 PM.

Feeding Solution. This consists of a solution of sugar and water. While ordinary white or brown sugar is satisfactory, you may also have good luck with a mixture of maple syrup and water. The taste of the maple syrup seems to stimulate many butterflies to feed; also, females seem to lay their full compliment of eggs and live out their maximum life span. A mixture of 5 parts syrup to 1 part water works well. In practice, a cotton pad is saturated with the feeding solution and laid on top of the cage. The butterfly usually finds the pad fairly quickly and will feed herself through the netting of the cage. Since the heat of the light tends to dry the pad, you must add water to the pad several times daily to keep it saturated. It is important to add water only, not sugar/water solution, as you do not want the concentration to become stronger and stronger. After three days (maximum) discard the old pad and replace it with a fresh one. Flowers can be used for food if desired, but this is not necessary for maintaining healthy butterflies.

Watering. Along with feeding it is very important to provide drinking water. This can be dome by spraying the whole cage and contents with a water mist several times daily. There are a wide variety of spray bottles or plant misters that will work for this. Usually the butterfly will start drinking the water as soon as you mist the cage. The water seems to help regulate body temperature, cleanse the digestive system, and most importantly to promote good egg production (since the ovae contain a high percentage of moisture). The mist on the foodplant also seems to help the female better recognize it and thus stimulates ovipositing.

Actual Care of Butterflies. Care of the female begins in the field at the time of collection. First, you want to try to select a good, healthy female. A female with a fat abdomen or one you actually observe ovipositing in the field is sure to give good results. A worn female with a slender abdomen is sure to have deposited her eggs already. After netting females in the field you will need a temporary holding cage. An ordinary brown paper lunch bag is the most convenient. Keep a supply of these folded bags in your field sack or your pocket until they are needed. Reach into your net with your forceps and get a hold of the female with her wings folded over her back. Place her in the bag using the forceps, and release her after you close the mouth of the bag around your forceps. Some collectors place the live butterflies in envelopes, but it appears the paper bag method is less traumatic and causes fewer injuries as the female will settle down quickly in the bag's darkness.

When you return home (or to your field camp), your first priority should be to feed the female(s). It is best to hand feed the females at this time to be absolutely certain that they feed. Get a cotton pad and saturate it with the sugar-water solution. Grasp the female by the base of the wings with either your fingers or forceps. Allow her front feet to touch the pad. Since butterflies taste with their feet, they will often begin feeding by themselves after coming into contact with the cotton pad. If the female refuses to feed, try uncoiling her proboscis with a teasing needle or insect pin and touch to the pad. Once you get the female to feed, cover her with a temporary cage while you get the foodplant prepared. While a small potted plant can be used, it is usually easier to cut small sprigs of foodplant and insert them into holes punched through the lid of a small, water-filled jar. The female will usually start depositing eggs on the third day after capture. Once egg laying begins, the foodplant should be changed every day if you want to obtain the maximum number of ova. This also prevents the female from damaging the eggs already laid by clawing them. After the eggs have been laid, it is generally inadvisable to attempt to remove them from the surface on which they were deposited., as many will be damaged and therefore never hatch. If they must be moved, leave them attached to a part of the substrate by cutting around them. If they are on leaves, cut around them. If they are on bark, cut out a piece with a razor blade. If they are on twigs, cut sections with pruning shears. If they are on the cage itself you will probably have to leave them until they hatch. Then the tiny larvae can be persuaded to crawl onto the foodplant, or they can be moved to the foodplant with the use of a small pointed paint brush (size #00 is good). If for some reason you must remove the ova from their substrate, first soften the adhesive with a small amount of water (use your paint brush) and then gently scrape them loose with a razor blade.

When the eggs hatch, place several leaves of the appropriate food plant into a plastic container (see Table 1 or 2, pp. 59-60). Make sure the leaves you use haven't been treated with a pesticide! Your container should have a screen or cheesecloth cover that prevents escape but provides adequate ventilation. If you use an airtight cover, moisture will build up and the leaves and larvae may mold. After the larvae start feeding, keep them supplied with ample amounts of fresh leaves. Remove any uneaten and dried leaves frequently. Keep the box in a warm and light place, but do not put them in direct sunlight!

If the larvae get large, or if you have many larvae, it may be necessary to transfer them to a larger container or to cages. Food plants may be placed in bottles of water to keep them fresh longer. Always stuff the neck of the bottle with tissue, paper toweling or cloth to keep the larvae from falling in the water and drowning. Provide fresh food, keep the container clean and uncrowded, and provide plenty of ventilation if you want your rearing efforts to succeed. To keep small sprigs of foodplant fresh, try a florist's waterpick (a small vial that has a rubber cap with a small hole in it). Another method that works well is making cuttings of the foodplant and placing them in yogurt cups containing water. The holes in the yogurt cup's cover should be just large enough for the stem of the cutting to fit through, otherwise the larvae may fall into the water. Then place the yogurt cups in a fishtank with a mesh screen covering it.

Do not disturb larvae once they have begun to spin cocoons or form chrysalises. You may need to supply them with sticks or other objects for chrysalis or cocoon attachment. At this point it is necessary to determine whether the species you are rearing overwinters (hibernates) in the pupal stage. This will determine whether the adults will emerge in a week or two, or whether the pupae (cocoons) must be exposed to cold temperatures before the adults emerge. Life cycle information for many common species of butterflies and moths is contained in Tables 2 and 3.

Gallon Jar Method for Rearing Lepidoptera.

A great deal of success has been reported with the use of gallon jars, like the type available in most restaurants and school kitchens, for raising caterpillars. Select jars that have tight fitting lids and an opening sufficiently large to get your hand into. Plastic jars will also work, but are less desirable because it is more difficult to observe what is going on inside.

The selected jar(s) should be thoroughly washed out and dried so that no foreign odors remain. A small amount of baking soda added to the rinse water will greatly assist in removing strange odors. After this process has been completed and the eggs are introduced, the cover may be left off until hatching occurs. Young larvae roam about, so as soon as they hatch out the lid must be put on and fresh food sprinkled with a few drops of distilled water added. The rearing jars must be kept out of the sun at all times. An ideal location is a well lit room with a southern exposure, with the jars placed on a north wall area. It is essential that excessive moisture be carefully controlled; if water condenses inside the jar the lid should be removed lust long enough for the moisture to evaporate.

Successful larval rearing depends upon uncrowded conditions. A large number of small larvae (up to 50) may be kept in one jar to start with, but as they grow larger they should be given additional room. The larger species, such as silkworm moths, should be limited to no more than 3 per jar as they approach maturity. The jars must be cleaned on a regular basis, but no more than every other day. The lid should be removed for about a half hour before cleaning; this lets the jar dry out and greatly facilitates the cleaning process. To clean adequately, empty the jar and wipe out carefully with paper toweling. If the larvae have to be moved while cleaning, they should never be handled directly but induced to move themselves from one leaf area to another. It is permissible to snip off some old leaf area and place this together with the larvae in the fresh material. Another reason for not forcibly removing larvae is that they may be going through the molting process and removing them at that particular time could be fatal.

Larvae should be given fresh food daily but do not crowd them with too much food. When selecting food sources extreme care should be taken that you are not feeding material from a chemically sprayed area, as this can immediately wipe out all your livestock in a few short hours. All collected leaves should be carefully inspected for other insects and spiders or egg sacs. Very few disease problems should be evident, but under crowded conditions or lack of sufficient food materials some species might attack one another and cause bleeding.

The following species have been reared successfully using the gallon jar method: cecropia (on red-osier dogwood and willow), luna moth (on walnut), promethea (on sassafras), polyphemus (on maple and birch), imperial moth (on maple), and atlas and Cynthia moth (on ailanthus). All of these leaves stayed fresh and crisp for several days when the lids are left on; the maple had a tendency to wilt sooner than the other tree species. This method can also be used for the monarch (on milkweed), black swallowtail (on Queen-Anne's-lace, or wild carrot), and the garden tiger (on dandelion).

Mature larvae may be left to spin their cocoons in the jars, or they may be placed into a cardboard shoebox with some dried twigs and leaves. If using the jars for spinning, the started cocoons should be removed before they are completely spun and placed onto a tray or cardboard box; this method assures the rearer of easier handling of the finished cocoons. The cocoons should not be disturbed for one week, after which time they can be moved to an unheated building or placed in a refrigerator (with the exception of atlas moth cocoons, which should be kept indoors).

Larval (Caterpillar) Foodplant Requirements

In order for the insect livestock breeder to have good success in rearing larvae, a knowledge of trees and other plants is necessary. Even if the very best rearing methods are used, a poor knowledge of food plants will hinder the breeder.

The list of preferred foodplants is long for some species, and short for others (see Tables 2 and 3). But even in the case of polyphytophagous species there is usually one prime foodplant, and survival rates are best when this plant is used. The problem is the prime foodplant preferred by larvae may vary in different areas, probably due to localized ancestry. Caterpillars possess a sense of "taste" and reject any fare deemed unsuitable. However, there is always a certain percentage (albeit, very small at times) that will survive on any of the allied foodplants listed for that species. Indeed, the way such a foodplant may have first been listed was by discovering a mature larva on the plant, but that observation does not reflect the survival rate and the many that might have perished on the same plant. Thus, in order for a high yield in rearing, the prime foodplant in the locality must be determined and used, even though the physical handling characteristics of the plant are not altogether suitable.

After a foodplant is accepted by the larvae, the discriminating factor breaks down to a certain degree, surely by the third instar, and perhaps by the second. This probably occurs because it is no longer needed, since in many species, once the foodplant is selected, the larvae are not likely to wander far. The choice, once made, stands, and the task of eating becomes foremost. Now an allied foodplant that has more favorable handling characteristics may be substituted for the original foodplant. Since some of these listed foodplants are seemingly unrelated, it is likely that there are various chemical constituents that fool the larvae's "tasting" mechanism in its partial state of degeneration, while most other plants are still rejected.

In this manner, a foodplant that stays fresher longer is substituted in order to decrease the work of rearing a great deal. More can be cared for in the same amount of time, and fewer eggs are required to start with because of the increased rate of survival. For example, this method works well with polyphemus, luna, and the royal walnut moth, all of which prefer walnut (at least in central and southern Maryland), but are easily switched to sweet gum, a prime rearing plant. Likewise, imperial moth larvae are known to feed on a variety of hardwoods, but in most areas both long and short needled pines are the prime foodplants, and since this plant stays fresh for long periods of time, it makes an ideal foodplant.

There are a few important things to remember in keeping branches fresh in water. Branches of most deciduous trees can be kept fresh for long periods. Always select a short branch and make a long diagonal cut. Trim off any long twigs, and keep them separately in water if desired. Ailanthus leaves keep better if the end of the stalk is crushed. It is best to place the branch in deep water in the shade. The second growth that comes up when a tree is cut down is very good for rearing larvae. Boxelder trees and other maples with large crops of seeds do not seem to have the food value of male trees or second growth. Willow, walnut, butternut, and hickory keep poorly in water.

When rearing exotic species, a batch of cocoons or eggs sometimes emerge unexpectedly in the fall. By rearing the larvae on a carefully chosen plant, they should be able to reach maturity. Certain northern trees and plants retain their leaves until late fall. Lilac, oak, willow, wild cherry, tuliptree, elderberry, and privet are among these. Variable success may be had by deep-freezing leaves for winter use. Evergreen plants such as oak and privet, are sometimes of great value. Cured and dried leaves can be made palatable by keeping them in high humidity. Larvae are often reluctant to accept such offerings, but can sometimes be induced to feed on them. Hard leaves like evergreen oak can be made more acceptable by presoaking to soften them. Lettuce can frequently be used as a starter for new larvae should the correct food plant not be immediately available.

Using a Turgorator. The turgorator is a recently developed device used to keep branches fresh for prolonged periods of time. A piece of soft plastic hose and a hose clamp are the only materials used. One end of the hose is attached to a water outlet and the other end to the cut-off branch of food plant with a diameter of approximately one-half inch (varying with the inner diameter of the hose). The pressure is then turned on to fill the hose with water while the clamp is tightened enough to stop the flow of water. It is important that no air is trapped between the water and the branch. The pressure will force the water into the leaves to such an extent that they will turn darker and water droplets will appear on the underside of the leaves. This pressure will also restore moisture to slightly wilted leaves. Branches will keep fresh in a bottle of water once they have been saturated with water. Freshness is maintained for as long as a week if the water level is kept above the end of the branch. The turgorator is especially useful in keeping plants such as willow or ash in a usable condition.

Pupation Time

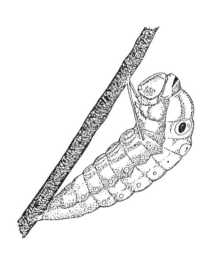

Butterflies generally have a naked pupae (chrysalis), which is attached to a plant (or side of a cage) by silk threads. Most moths, on the other hand, spin an elaborate cocoon of silk around the pupa. However, some moths, such as sphinx moths, pupate in the ground. After the last molt the larvae should be transferred to a container that has several inches of peat moss in the bottom. The mature larvae will crawl into the moss and can be left in the moss until they emerge on their own.

Table 2. Quick Helps for Butterfly Rearing

Butterfly Species	Larval Food Plants	Days to maturity: Egg	Larva
American copper	sorrel	4	14
American painted lady	everlasting	3-5	21
Baltimore	turtlehead	21	H*
Buckeye	plantain, Gerardia	5	14
Cabbage butterfly	cabbage, collards, broccoli, winter cress	5-6	14
Comma	elm, nettles, hops	5-7	21
Common sulphur	clover, vetch, trefoil, alfalfa	5-6	21
East. black swallowtail	carrots, parsley, parsnip, celery, Queens Anne's lace/wild carrot	5-7	24
Great spangled fritillary	violets	3-4	14
Hackberry butterfly	hackberry	4	30
Milbert's tortoise shell	nettles	4-5	14
Monarch	milkweed, dogbane	7	10
Mourning cloak	willow, poplar, elm, hackberry	14	21
Painted lady	thistles, nettles	4-5	21
Questionmark	elm, nettles, hops	5-7	21
Red admiral	nettles	4-5	21
Spicebush swallowtail	spicebush, sweet bay, sassafras, prickly ash	5-7	21
Tiger swallowtail	cherry, ash, birch, lilac, aspen, willow, hornbeam	5-7	22
Viceroy	willow, poplar, birch, cherry	4-5	18

(* = hibernates before emerging)

Table 3. Quick Helps for Moth Rearing

Moth Species	Larval Food Plants	Days to Maturity: Egg	Larva
Abbot's sphinx	grape, woodbine	7+	35
Achemon sphinx	grape, Virginia creeper	7+	35
Bumblebee sphinx moth	vibernum, snowberry, hawthorne	7	35-42
Cecropia moth	apple, willow, maple, cherry, lilac, boxelder	10	60
Cynthia moth	ailanthus, cherry, willow, ash	7	42
Four-horned sphinx	elm	7	35
Garden tiger moth	dandelion, plantain, dock	7	56
Imperial moth	elm, spruce, pine, cherry, maple, birch, alder, hickory	13	42
Io moth	willow, cherry, oak, hickory, plum, elm, ash, poplar, tuliptree, basswood	10+	40
Laurel sphinx	privet	7	35
Luna moth	beech, walnut, birch, oak, willow, hickory,	15	48+
Nessus sphinx	grape, Virginia creeper	7	35
Oak silk moth	oak, crabapple, hawthorn	7	28+
Pandora's sphinx	grape, Virginia creeper	7	35
Pen mark sphinx	ash, cherry	7+	40
Pink spotted sphinx	sweet potato	7+	40
Polyphemus moth	elm, maple, cherry, oak, basswood, apple, boxelder, hickory, birch, butternut	7	48
Promethea moth	cherry, sassafras, willow, poplar, ash, apple, pear, lilac, plum	11	42
Tobacco hornworm	tobacco, tomato	7	40+
Tomato hornworm	tomato, potato	7	40+
Twin-spotted sphinx	apple, elm, ash, willow, birch	6	30
Underwing moths (Catocala)	plum, apple, cherry, willow	var	H*
Virgo tiger moth	dandelion, plantain	?	49
White-lined sphinx	grape, apple, dock, chickweed, purslane, willow	6	30

(* = hibernates before emerging)

Collecting and Caring for Silkmoth Cocoons

Three of the species of giant silkmoths (the cecropia, polyphemus and promethea) generally spin their cocoons attached to tree limbs or bushes, which makes them fairly easy to find. The cocoons of other species, like the Luna and Io (occasionally polyphemus) are spun on the ground and are extremely difficult to locate.

Promethea. Cocoons of this species are most often found on lilac, wild cherry and sassafras, but may occasionally be found on poplar and

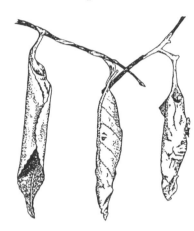

birch. These trees are common along fence rows, railroad tracks and road sides. The bulky female moths are not stunt fliers, and in fact have a difficult time moving through thick vegetation. For this reason the eggs are usually deposited on those trees along the outer edges of woods, marshes and bogs. There is a high preference for young trees and small shrubs, and isolated trees are also a favorite. Spotting cocoons is only a matter of knowing what to look for. Promethea cocoons look like a leaf that did not fall off the tree in autumn. The cocoon is usually wrapped in a leaf which the larva pulled around itself as it spun the cocoon. It is about a half inch in diameter and one to two inches long, and is always hanging vertically from the twig or branch. This makes it easier to realize it's a cocoon even when you are several yards away. If you find one cocoon, you can bet that there are at least several others nearby or even in the same tree.

Polyphemus and Cecropia. These two species of silk moths are more common in urban areas than the previous species. Both species feed on birch, willow, maple, lilac, fruit trees, and many other landscape trees and shrubs. Polyphemus cocoons are larger than promethea cocoons and are jellybean-like in shape. They also camouflage their cocoons by incorporating leaves into the structure. Cecropia cocoons are even larger and may either be a rather tough, compact structure, or loosely spun (in which case it may have a diameter in excess of three inches). These loosely spun cocoons are usually spun nearer the ground than the compact type common in trees and shrubs. Both types are attached lengthwise to the branch or twig (and therefore do not hand vertically).

Proper Care of Silkmoth Cocoons. During the winter months it is important to store moth cocoons someplace where it is cold. This is necessary for proper development of the adult moth. Pupae (cocoons) can be stored in any protected place that is exposed to cold temperatures, such as a breezeway, garage, porch or outdoor rearing cage. Many species will respond to a short "artificial" winter and so some people store cocoons in the refrigerator (or as previously mentioned, in an unheated garage, shed or breezeway). Place the cocoons and a single green leaf (to maintain proper moisture) into a container and put the container in the refrigerator for 8 to 12 weeks. Cocoons kept in the refrigerator are often subject to desiccation and should be occasionally sprinkled with water. A good sprinkler can be made from any bottle with a spray atomizer (be sure to rinse the bottle thoroughly before using).

If you want the adults to emerge from their cocoons earlier than they normally would, bring them indoors from the cold or remove them from the refrigerator early. It is too much of a shock to bring the pupae in from the cold to room temperature in one step. One should try to provide the pupae with a natural environment and warm them gradually to room temperature over a period of one to two weeks.

Inside of the cocoon in the air space around the pupa is a microenvironment that has to have the right amount of heat and moisture to keep the pupa healthy. Humidity is important. Without the proper humidity the silk threads are hard to penetrate and the moth often cannot emerge. The dry heated air of a home is not good for a moth cocoon and it is sometimes more than the moth can stand. To help the pupa adjust, sprinkle a few drops of water on the cocoon twice a day for about a week after bringing the cocoons inside. Another method is to place the cocoon on a moist sponge, but beware of mold! Either way the moisture will penetrate and soften the silk.

Preparing for Adult Emergence. One more thing to remember when caring for moth cocoons. Put the cocoon in a container with fibrous sidewalls, such as a box. Punch small air holes in the box. It is also a good idea to attach cheesecloth or screening to the sides and top (to provide a foothold for the adult to hang from while their wings expand). The emerging moth must be in a vertical position after emerging so that gravity will act on its new wings and aid in expansion. Do not disturb the emerging adults until the wings appear to be fully expanded and hardened; this usually takes 24 to 48 hours.

Once the butterflies or moths have emerged, you may want to release it (native species only!) or keep it for further breeding. If you choose to keep it you will need a cage made of netting or a similar material (see figure on page 53). Old lampshades make an excellent frame that can be covered with netting, or you can make the frame out of wood. For a minimal expense it is even possible to build a screen house of 2x4s and garden netting (used to keep birds off berries). Caged butterflies may obtain food (nectar) from flowers provided inside the cage, or from sugar-water solutions (on cotton or in butterfly feeder), or from sliced fruits (apples, peaches, banana, etc.).

The great spangled fritillary, Speyeria cybele

BLACK SWALLOWTAIL
(Papilio polyxenes)

Background Information

The black swallowtail butterfly is a large, colorful butterfly commonly found almost everywhere in North America east of the Rocky Mountains. The caterpillars, pupae and adult are all attractive in appearance and show interesting behaviors. The larvae show specialized behavioral traits that are especially impressive.

Biology and Life Cycle

The life cycle has four distinct stages: egg, larva, pupa and adult. The larva feeds of a range of plants in the carrot family including carrot, wild carrot (Queen-Anne's-lace), celery, parsnips, and parsley. The winter is passed in the pupal stage, in diapause. This diapause is facultative, and can be controlled by manipulating photoperiod and temperature. Under appropriate conditions the life cycle is relatively short, requiring six to seven weeks for completion.

Rearing Instructions

Livestock to start a culture can be easily obtained from numerous dealers or by field collection of either adults or larvae. To obtain eggs, mated female butterflies are closely confined over parsley leaves. Parsley makes an excellent food source as it is cheaply and easily available in grocery stores. The eggs are laid directly on the leaves and can be removed with their bits of leaf for storage until hatching occurs. Newly hatched larvae are transferred to cut bunches of fresh parsley in rearing cages or other suitable containers. No more than thirty larvae should be kept in a cage and the cages should be cleaned daily. The larvae may be kept at ordinary room temperature (70°F or slightly above).

Mature larvae should be allowed to pupate on the side of the cage and then removed. Diapause in the pupal stage is controlled by rearing larvae under different lighting regiments. Larvae exposed to at least 16 hours of light per day develop into non-diapausing pupae; larvae exposed to only ten hours of light per day develop into diapausing pupae. Diapausing pupae can be kept in good condition for long periods when stored at a temperature under 40°F in open containers, as long as they are not allowed to become dehydrated. A refrigerator with an open container of water is sufficient storage.

If pupae are not needed right away they can be left in cold storage for long periods of time and then brought back to normal room temperature. In general, the longer a pupa has been chilled, the shorter will be the time required to produce an adult butterfly after removal from the cold. After about three months of cold storage an adult will emerge from the pupae within 2-3 weeks after removal from the cold. Lengthening the period of cold exposure (up to about 12 months) does not harm the pupa, but the length of time for emergence to occur is not further reduced.

Whenever adult butterflies emerge they should be put into large flight cages, fed on a sugar-water solution, and kept until wanted for mating. Since the black swallowtail will not carry out natural courtship and mating behavior in captivity, hand-pairing must be used to obtain matings and a new generation of eggs. Fresh, vigorous adults should be chosen - one of each sex. Hold one butterfly in each hand, with their heads directed away from each other. Bring the tips of the abdomens towards each other; as contact is make this should induce the pair of butterflies to initiate copulation.

ANISE SWALLOWTAIL
(Papilio zelicaon)

Background Information
This is a fairly common swallowtail found west of the Rocky
Mountains. The larvae of zelicaon are very easy to rear and they grow
remarkably fast. They can be raised in screen cages on cut stems of
fennel. They like sunlight and warmth so you can put the cage on a window
ledge. The larvae are like most swallowtails in that they look like bird
droppings for the first few instars until they assume their distinctive
color patterns.

Rearing Instructions
Foodplant. The larvae are collected on wild fennel, but his is by no
means the only hostplant. In fact, almost any plants in the family
Umbelliferae (parsley, dill, carrots, etc.) will work. It has even been
reported that zelicaon will eat citrus. It is very common for this
swallowtail to migrate into the city in the summer and breed in suburban
herb gardens.

Assuming you are starting with freshly emerged adults the first task
is to get a mating. Luckily, swallowtails are very easy to hand-pair and
this is probably the only way you are going to get a mating. Hand-pairing
is one of those things best learned by observing someone else rather than
reading about it, but it is not difficult, and once seen it takes very
little time to get the hang of it. Here are some helpful hints though:
(1) Feed them twice a day with a honey-water solution (20% honey and 80%
water) and allow them to flutter around in the sunlight; (2) Make sure you
rinse the tip of the abdomen in water after feeding to prevent the
genitalia from becoming clogged; (3) Do not attempt pairing until the
butterflies are at least one day old; (4) Do not attempt a pairing just
after you have fed them or they will defecate all over each other rather
than mate; and (5) Don't be discouraged if they do not mate the first time
you try. Sometimes it takes a few days before they are ready, and many
breeders have their best luck when the swallowtails are three days old.
The pair should stay together for at least 20 minutes for you to consider
the mating successful. If they pull apart after a few minutes, try again!

By now, hopefully, you have a gravid female. Getting them to lay eggs
is not very difficult. Set them up in a small screen cage with a few
living sprigs of their hostplant. The cage should be just large enough
for them to flap around a bit, but small enough so they are in constant
contact with their hostplant. This is very important as too large a cage
and not enough hostplant may not provide enough stimuli for them to lay.
Once this is accomplished, put the cage in a warm, sunny spot.
Swallowtails need a lot of sunlight and warmth to elicit egg laying.
Continue to feed them twice a day until you have got all the eggs you want
or until the butterfly finally dies. If your little prisoner does not lay
within 3 or 4 days then try arranging the hostplant differently in her
cage. Some swallowtails like to lay on the undersides of overhanging
branches so you could try hanging some hostplant from the roof of the
cage. If this does not work then you either have the wrong hostplant, a
fickle female, or she may not be fertile.

When they are ready to pupate, they will attach themselves to the
foodplant of the side of the cage with a support strand of silk and become
inactive. Do not disturb them until they have molted into the chrysalis
and the chrysalis has hardened. These butterflies are multiple brooded in
many areas so keep an eye on your chrysalis. If it does not hatch within
a month or so it is probably going to hold off until next spring.

Diapause. P. zelicaon diapauses in the pupal stage. As mentioned earlier, there are many populations that are multiple brooded. The techniques described under the black swallowtail will probably work for this species as well.

Special Notes. Like most swallowtail larvae, P. zelicaon emit a foul smell from their osmeteria (those orange horns on the head) when disturbed. Keep this in mind if you have a sensitive nose!

KOREAN CITRUS BUTTERFLY
(Papilio xuthus)

Background Information

The Korean citrus butterfly is well established in Hawaii and makes a good candidate for rearing. It can be found on foliage of various citrus trees (lime, lemon, orange, etc.).

The eggs are laid singly and are a pale green color, darkening with age. The 1st instar larvae are rather stiffly bristled and very active, moving at a high rate of speed from place to place. Next the larvae takes on a "bird dropping" coloration, with splotches of brownish-gray. In the final instar the caterpillar takes on the traditional green swallowtail coloration. Pupation requires about 15 days.

The feeding by these caterpillars is rather odd, as there is no bulk consumption of the foliage. The larvae remains in the center of the leaf and sucks the juice from the midvein. In only a few rare instances will small pieces of foliage be consumed. The adult butterfly feeds on nectar, seeming to prefer Bougainvillea.

The techniques described for other swallowtails apply to this species as well.

FRITILLARY BUTTERFLIES
(Speyeria spp.)

Background Information

Some species of Speyeria can be difficult to rear. Some are apparently restricted to one species of violet, and may be difficult to rear on local species of violet. The more common or widespread fritillaries are often the easiest to rear, since they have greater tolerances to temperatures, humidity, foodplants, crowding, etc. Some larvae may die from viral infections or desiccation, but perserverence and practice with improve your success rate.

Rearing Instructions

To collect ova from a female fritillary, collect a slightly worn female (this increases the chance of getting a mated female). Mating takes place very soon after the female emerges, so a very fresh female in likely to have not mated yet. Also, the females with more swollen abdomens naturally lay the most ova, so try to select a "fat" specimen if you are able to choose from several.

Fritillary

Most breeders place the female into a paper sack set in partial shade. A small wire screen sleeve, or cage with nylon netting across the top works better. The cage can be set on a smooth surface, which will prove useful later. It is not necessary to place violets in the cage, as the female will deposit ova on the screen and the netting.

It is very important to feed the female butterfly on a daily basis. Make a solution of sugar or syrup and distilled water, and fill a vial cap with it. Carefully grasp the ventral thorax of the female with thumb and index finger and use a toothpick or pin to unroll her proboscis into the sugar solution. She usually will immediately feed on her own and will continue feeding until she is full (which often takes about 10 minutes). When she is done, she will withdraw and recoil her proboscis. At this point wash her proboscis and legs under lukewarm tap water from a faucet. This prevents the sugar solution from drying, which may inhibit movement in future feeding attempts.

The female fritillary may live for several weeks in the cage, if properly fed, and will lay several hundred eggs. When she dies, or before the eggs begin to hatch, place the entire cage into a clear plastic bag large enough to accommodate it and use a twist-tie to close the bag. Eggs laid on the smooth substrate base can be carefully scraped off with a razor blade after a few days. Depending on the species of Speyeria, eggs will often hatch in two weeks or less.

After hatching, transfer the tiny larvae to large petri dishes (no more than 50 larvae per dish) with a small artist's paint brush. A piece of filter paper placed in the bottom of the petri dish will absorb moisture from the feces of the caterpillars. Choose young, tender violet leaves cut with about 2cm of stem, wrap the leaves in cotton and wet the cotton with distilled water. Change the filter paper daily and replace the violets every two days. A 25- to 40-watt light bulb should be suspended about 50cm above the petri dishes (a tall gooseneck lamp works fine) and left continuously on. This induces feeding and the larvae won't go into diapause as they would in nature. The larvae can be kept in the dishes until the 2nd or 3rd instar, at which time they should be transferred to another type of cage.

For rearing the larvae to the pupal stage, use 3 lb coffee cans, filled within 8 cm of the top with sand, and then covered with 5 cm of crushed peat moss. Put the violet stems in small vials (6 cm tall x 1.5 cm wide). The coffee can easily holds three or four vials filled with cut violets. Cut the violet leaves about 7 cm below the leaf and insert as many as the vial will hold. Fill the vial with distilled water (a polyethylene wash bottle works great) and push the vial into the peat until the top of the vial is level with the surface of the peat. The same cage that was used for the female can be used for the larvae, and fits into the coffee can. Replace violets when necessary, being careful not to disturb the pupating larvae. Larvae may pupate on the nylon mesh, on the screen, under violet leaves silked together, or under the peat moss. They always hang by their cremaster.

If you wish to transfer the pupae to an emergence cage, scrape off the silken area around the base of the pupa with a razor blade, then tape it to your emergence cage. Pupation often lasts two weeks, but also varies between species. A good emergence temperature is 75-80°F with 70% relative humidity.

ROYAL WALNUT MOTH
(Citheronia regalis)

Rearing Instructions

The larvae of the royal walnut moth, almost known as the hickory
horned devil, may be reared on walnut foliage. However, walnut wilts in a
days time (unless cut diagonally with a razor blade above the thick base
and immediately dipped in water, in which case it might last two days),
and requires constant attention. Fourth instar larvae may be safely
transferred to sumac (which keeps about a week in water) and fifth instar
larvae may be safely switched to sweetgum (which keeps about two weeks in
water).

When the caterpillars reach maturity they shrivel and wander, during
which time they may burrow at whim. Clay is too hard a medium and sand is
too soft. A general medium is moist tumbled peat moss 6 inches deep. No
more than four larvae of equal development should be placed per square
foot of medium. Any that come to the surface after burrowing may be
sprinkled with peat to cover. They should not be disturbed for one month,
at which time they should be carefully dug up and inspected. One of the
primary imperfections among pupae is the inability to remove the head
capsule and perfectly cement the head, legs, and antennae into a uniformly
smooth capsule. The survivors should be stored in comparatively crowded
quarters in moist sphagnum moss. The acidity of the moss retards mold.

Placing the pupae outside is tricky business because they are not in
the same conditions as the wild population protected under the soil.
Pupae freeze to death at 10°-15°F, and exposure to balmy temperatures
in the spring will cause unnaturally early emergence. They keep well in
pans of sphagnum moss lightly covered with plastic wrap, stacked in a
refrigerator at approximately 33-35°F. They should be checked regularly
to guard against dehydration. Examine them once a month at room
temperature, removing any that become excessively soft. They should
respond to gentle pressure by movement of the abdomen, often hard to
notice in some individuals. Clean off any mold with a soft toothbrush and
put them back in the refrigerator within an hour after removal.

In the spring (early to late May depending on latitude), bring the pans outside and place them in a secure cage in a shady location. The adults should emerge sometime in July, during the hatching period of the wild population. In warm weather the danger of mold is greatest, so keep an eye on the pupae.

Mating the adults is a tricky proposition. The best chances are in attracting wild males, or releasing the captive males and letting them come back on their own.

COMMON WILD SILKMOTHS
(Hyalophora, Antherea, Actias, Samia, and Callosamia species)

Background Information
In nature, larvae are under tremendous lethal pressure at all times. Predators (both insect and other animals), disease, weather, and atmospheric conditions all take their toll. By rearing, it is possible to eliminate predators outright and protect against bad weather. Therefore, it should be your objective to rear larvae under conditions that will not lead to disease outbreak.

Rearing Instructions
The eggs should be placed in containers soon after they have been laid. Place twenty eggs to a half-gallon cardboard container. These are light and durable, but plastic boxes will also work well. The container should be kept out of the sun at all times to avoid condensation. Room temperature is right for normal development of the embryo. Watch for the larvae to emerge soon after the eggs turn dark. Ten to fifteen days is the normal incubation time, although some may hatch in a weeks time under optimal conditions. Place fresh plants in the container as soon as the larvae appear. If the container is airtight, the leaves will keep much longer. The container should be kept clean and the condensation wiped off regularly. Change the leaves as soon as they become too dry. In changing leaves, do not handle the larvae or attempt to pry them off of the leaf or twigs. Cut away the section of the leaf on the which the larvae is resting. In about four days the larvae will prepare for their first molt. The larva will spin a small pad of silk which is necessary for molting. Molting larvae are slightly paler in color. Learn to recognize molting caterpillars so they will not be mistaken for diseased larvae or disturbed. Most silk moth larvae (Saturniidae) shed their skins four times, occasionally five. This is always a delicate stage of development. If an older larva becomes detached from its pad of silk, it may be able to shed its skin if placed on a piece of cheesecloth. This process is continued until the larvae are about one inch long.

There are three methods to finish rearing the larvae: rearing in containers, sleeving out, and setting out larvae with no protection.

Containers. Rearing in containers and cages is probably the most common method, especially if only a few larvae are to be reared. No matter what kind of container or cage you use, the food plant should be kept in a bottle of water to ensure freshness. If the container is airtight, only a few larvae should be reared together, otherwise disease might appear and wipe them all out in a short time. The best conditions for all species are as follows: good circulation of air; relatively low humidity (about 60%); fresh food plant; and, clean, uncrowded conditions. Keep these criteria in mind when selecting containers and container location for rearing.

Sleeving Out. Sleeving out is probably the best method of rearing larvae. A bag of cheesecloth, or any similar material, can be used. One branch or a small tree may be sleeved depending on the number of larvae to be reared. A bag six feet long and three feet in diameter works well. If the sleeve is too small, the larvae will eat all the leaves overnight. A general rule would be not to sleeve more than two or three larvae per leaved foot of branch. Always shake the branch vigorously before putting on the sleeve to dislodge predatory insects and spiders. Since the larvae are being reared on live trees, they are under the most natural conditions possible. Because of this you will probably rear out larger larvae when sleeving out than with any other method. There are some disadvantages. If wasps or birds discover larvae in a sleeve, they may chew or peck their way inside. Weather may kill larvae not native to the region.

Setting Out. Setting out is certainly the easiest method to rear larvae. In order to have success, large numbers of larvae must be set out where parasites, birds, and other natural enemies are least abundant. Such areas are usually in the suburbs of cites. Also, the areas must not be sprayed with insecticides! The best trees are about 10 feet tall, free of bird's nests, away from excessive weed growth, and not in danger of being cut down. If the larvae are hand raised to about 1 inch or more before setting out, they will have a better chance of survival. It is possible, however, to have good success when setting out the ova directly. After moths have finished laying in paper sacks, paper disks covered with groups of 10-20 eggs can be cut out and stapled to the undersides of the correct host plant. Species than wander when spinning, or that are not native to the area should be reared in captivity. Those larvae which suffer from extensive parasite attack should be collected soon after the last molt. The eggs of tachinid fly parasites are generally laid on the outside of the body and can be removed by gently scrapping with a dull knife. If this is done before any of the parasite eggs have hatched, the larva will live. When the fly eggs have hatched, dark spots will be visible under the skin of the caterpillar where the fly larvae are feeding.

Overwintering. Most of our native silk moths can tolerate the most severe winters and emerge normally the next summer. Some species from the southwest should be overwintered in above-freezing temperatures, although an occasional frost does not hurt them. All species can be kept under refrigeration at 40°F. The cocoons should be chilled from late October until late April. It is best to make transfers gradually.

Emergence. Difficulty is rarely encountered in this phase of rearing. If cocoons are to emerge at a normal time, they should be placed out of doors, in a screened porch. If they are to be hatched during the winter, they can be exposed to room temperature after at least 6 weeks of chilling. If the indoor environment is excessively dry, spray the cocoons with a small amount of water on a weekly basis.

One of the best emergence cages that there is can be made from the frame of an old lampshade. Cover the metal framework with screen. The bottom and top should be wood or masonite. The top is removable and extends over the edge to provide essential shade from the sun. The slanting sides are superior to either vertical or horizontal planes in that the moth can spread its wings more easily.

TULIP-TREE SILKMOTH
(Callosamia angulifera)

Background Information
In many areas of the southeastern United States Callosamia angulifera is double brooded (2 generations per year). Moths of the first brood can be taken as early as mid-May and early June. Both the male and female moths are attracted to lights. The males seem to come to lights about 11:00 PM and the females come mostly between 1:00 AM and 5:00 AM. If you want to attract female angulifera to lights you have to be up long before sunrise. The bright orange-brown females are easily spotted by both birds and humans alike at dawn.

Collecting wild cocoons is not an easy job. Most cocoons spun on the foodplant will fall to the ground and are very hard to locate. Also, larvae prefer to feed on the uppermost portions of the foodplant and prefer large mature, trees to small, young ones. For this reason collecting wild larvae is also almost impossible.

Rearing Instructions
After a female moth is obtained, it is best to place her in a large brown paper bag for egg laying. The eggs of C. angulifera are very similar to those of C. promethea in size, shape and color; however, incubation time is much different. Promethea ovae hatch in 8 to 11 days, while angulifera eggs require 14 to 18 days. The young larvae are very tiny, yellow with black heads. When the larvae hatch they must be given food very quickly and if not fed with 16 hours they may die. The tuliptree (Liriodendron tulipifera) is the preferred host, with sassafras (Sassafras albidum) as a second choice. Cherry or plum (Prunus spp.) can also be used, but should only be used when tuliptree or sassafras is not available. Newly hatched larvae have a tendency to wander, even when put directly on tuliptree leaves. C. angulifera larvae are very susceptible to viral diseases, so cage sanitation is of absolute importance. After the larvae complete their final instar, they will begin constructing their thin paper-like cocoons. The cocoon is usually rather oval-shaped and resembles that of the luna moth, Actias luna. Cocoons may be spun on the foodplant or on the ground.

ATLAS MOTH
(Attacus atlas formosanus)

Background Information
The Atlas moth is a tropical species that can be raised in captivity even in the temperate regions of the United States. Ovae must be obtained from other breeders.

Rearing Instructions
The eggs are 2.5mm in diameter and cream-colored with purple-brown stains.

After hatching from the eggs, the caterpillars grow quickly and feed on leaves of ailanthus (Chinese Tree of Heaven), lilac, ash, sassafras, privet, cherry, rhododendron, mountain laurel, apple, and willow. The larvae will need plenty of fresh leaves and an occasional misting with water. The caterpillars will drink droplets of water from the foliage and side of the cage. Remove uneaten foliage and keep the cage clean.

At first the caterpillars are yellowish-white and are covered with rows of spines. Their color very much resembles the color of newly-hatched promethea larvae. For the first month the caterpillars may eat little, but as they grow larger they eat more. Maturing larvae are fat and translucent blue-green with freckles of the same color but darker on the segments behind the head, on the legs, on the prolegs, and on the lower sides of the body. After each molt the caterpillar covers its body with a white powder. This powder hides the true color, but it wears off before the next molt (or at least most of it) as it is loosely put on the body. If a branch bearing a caterpillar is jolted, there is generally a miniature snowstorm under the caterpillar as the powder falls. By the time the caterpillars mature they will reach a length of 4.5 to 6 inches.

When the larvae show signs of slacking off in their eating, it won't be long before cocoons begin to appear. The cocoons appear small compared to the larvae that formed them. The cocoons are wrapped in at least one leaf, which is attached to the branch by a strong peduncle. The cocoon is tan in color and egg shaped (about the size of a chicken egg). There is an evident escape "hatch" at the top of the cocoon. They are very tough and very heavy.

Pupation lasts about a month and the emerging moths frequently reach a wingspan of eight to nine inches!

PAMINA SILKMOTH
(Automeris pamina)

Background Information
This is a very pretty little saturniid is from southern Arizona and New Mexico. The larvae have been collected on oak in the wild, but may also be found larvae on mountain mahogany (Cercocarpus) and black locust (Robinia). It is entirely possible that they will accept many other plants. Plum would be a good try for those who feel so inclined.

Rearing Instructions
The larvae are generally collected from evergreen oak in the wild and can be switched over to deciduous oak in captivity. The larvae offered no resistance in switching and actually seemed to prefer the more tender leaves of the deciduous oak. The larvae are reared at room temperature in plastic boxes 2'x2'x8" at 50 larvae per box. The larvae are gregarious in all instars so they can handle a bit of crowding. A layer of paper towels was placed in the bottom of the box to absorb excess moisture. The boxes were cleaned every day or two (every day when they hit fourth instar) and new food and paper towels were put in. The leaves were lightly sprinkled with water so that the larvae could drink. Note: These larvae like to drink, so if you are rearing them under dry conditions and having problems, try sprinkling them with water occasionally. As the larvae spun their cocoons they were removed to a paper bag for storage.

The thin, papery cocoon is the diapausing stage and these should be stored in a cool place for the winter. When you are ready for your moths to emerge in the spring, start watering the cocoons regularly. The summer rains are what help break diapause in the wild. These moths are doubled brooded, so don't be surprised if your first set of cocoons starts to hatch in mid-summer. Flight times in Arizona tend to be May and July.

Special Notes. The larvae of A. pamina are beautiful black and white caterpillars but they have the typical stinging spines that most Automeris larvae possess **so handle with care!!!** Also, females are larger than males and female larvae have additional instars.

-71-

ILLUSTRIS SILKMOTH
(Automeris illustris)

Background Information

The genus Automeris (family Saturniidae) contains a number of mainly tropical species. The moths have conspicuous eyespots on the hindwing, the majority being vividly colored, and the larvae have poisonous spines. They are great fun to rear.

Automeris illustris is distributed from Brazil to Panama and can be successfully reared. Since A. illustris is a tropical species it is best to rear them in a heated insectary or cage which is maintained at about 25°C (80°F). The small larvae, until the third instar, can be kept in plastic boxes. Thereafter they may be reared in cages 18 inches square by 24 inches high. A cage this size will hold about a hundred larvae up to full size and pupation.

Rearing Instructions

Eggs and egg-laying. The eggs are laid in bunches, usually in captivity about 200 eggs are laid although dissection proves that the potential egg production is far greater than this. The moths lay freely on the sides of the cages, from which it is awkward to remove the eggs which are attached by a very strong cement. While it is more convenient to have moths lay in a cardboard box lined with paper, this does not work well for this species. Like all Automeris eggs, a black micropyle becomes visible a day or two after laying, provided they are fertile. Infertile eggs are laid in irregular clumps and soon shrivel up. The eggs are rather shiny white, show no color changes during development, and at 25°C hatch in about a week.

Larvae. After hatching, the larvae partly consume their eggshells. They then rest for over 24 hours and spend a further day or two wandering around in columns before settling to the serious business of feeding. During the first two instars they are yellowish in color tinged with brown. In the third instar they assume their final coloration, a uniform pale green, a white lateral line, orange spiracles, and white speckled brown markings round the legs ventrally.

Keep the early instars in plastic boxes and give them fresh food daily. After the third molt transfer them to cut foliage in bottles of water, the necks being tightly plugged with facial tissue to prevent the larvae from drowning themselves. In the early instars the larvae, which are very gregarious, spin a communal silk pad on which to molt. In later instars they tend to scatter more and the final two molts often take place on a leaf spun into a rough shelter. The larvae have eight instars and the period of feeding is 8 - 11 weeks at 25°C, the final instar being the most variable in length.

There is an inclination for the larvae to drop and wriggle when disturbed. Care must be taken that they do not escape by this means when being fed. Even more care should be taken not to come in contact with them, for their sting is painful (more so than that of the more familiar Io (bullseye) moth, Automeris io Fabricius). The poisonous spines are longer and finer than those of A. io and normally the larvae rest with these sloping upwards and forwards. When a larva is disturbed "its hackles rise", so to speak, and the spines are fanned upright and sideways.

The larvae are fond of eating fabric and it is essential to keep them in cages covered with metal.

Foodplants. The larvae are polyphytophagous on a variety of deciduous and broad-leaved evergreen trees. You may find a difference in size between those fed on plums (Malus spp.) and beech (Fagus sylvaticus) and those fed on Holme oak (Quercus ilex). The young larvae should be started off on rather fresh foliage and although the larger larvae readily accept privet (Ligustrum spp.), newly hatched larvae do so with reluctance and some mortality results.

Pupation. Normally the larvae pupate inside a tough silken cocoon spun up between the leaves, which are closely folded around it. However, the use of temperate zone foodplants for tropical species often means the leaves are too small. The normal situation is also aggravated in captivity by the population density and consequent disturbances in cages. In these circumstances illustris goes downward to spin its cocoon in the corners of the cage and one excellent way of gathering them up is to put crumpled newspaper and pieces of shaped pulpboard as used for packing eggs onto the floor of the cage and the cocoons will then be spun in there.

Diapause. In parts of tropical South America, A. illustris appears to be continuously brooded. In temperate regions the situation is somewhat obscure. When reared at 14-16 hours light, emergence of moths occurs 1-2 months after pupation. However, if larvae are reared with less than 12 hours of light per day many will enter diapause and emerge 4-5 months later.

Pairing. Unlike the Io moth, which is always easy to pair, A. illustris may prove difficult. Keep the moths in a large airy cage, with no more than several pairs. Actual copulation lasts only about half an hour and usually takes place four hours after sunset.

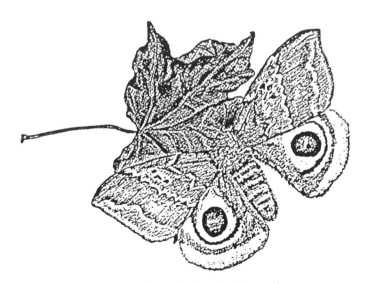

Io moth of North America

INDIAN OWL MOTH
(Dictyoploca simla)

Background Information
This moth is native to India and is generally quite easy to rear. The eggs of this species overwinter unhatched, and resemble small rugby balls. Their color is grayish-brown. The adult moths are generally colored gray and the forewing has a small eyespot and the hindwing has a larger, black-ringed eyespot. The thorax is colored light brown and grayish-brown. The male is nearly identical to the female, except for a deeper coloring and slimmer body.

Rearing Instructions
Place the ova in a small plastic box and put them in a cool place during the winter months. In the spring the larvae should hatch. The larvae will do well on hawthorne, but will also eat weeping willow, pear and apple leaves. They are extremely active in the first and second instars, and black with shiny heads. In the third instar their ground color is yellow with white hairs. The hairs are quite long and bushy, and very soft to the touch. There may also be a slight amount of gray hair on some larvae. In the final instar the hairs become greenish or bluish. The sides of their body are creamy with bluish-white dorsal bands along the body. The head is yellow with white hairs.

When the larvae are fully grown they will spin their cocoons. The cocoons are rather unusual, much like a fishing net and brown in color. After spinning the larvae enter the cocoons, seal them, and pupate within the closed mesh. Place the cocoons in a well aerated box and mist them occasionally to prevent desiccation. Since the pupae can be seen inside the cocoons, they are easily checked for disease.

CAJA TIGER MOTH
(Arctia caja)

Background Information
This tiger moth is infrequently taken as an adult in some areas, but the larvae are very common in the spring. Only about 2% of the caterpillars reach adulthood! The mature or nearly mature larvae can be found in the early summer. They feed on almost anything, but they are most frequently found on honeysuckle and cotoneaster.

Rearing Instructions
In captivity they may be fed buffalo bean and dandelion, and as a last resort, lettuce. The high water content of lettuce makes the frass very messy.

The cocoon are very flimsy, and often the pupae fall out. Thus, larvae can be removed as soon as they begin the shrink and placed on a cotton batting "bed" so they will not be deformed. If left on a hard surface, the soft pupae will flatten out. The pupae stay soft for around twelve hours, before finally hardening.

Adults emerge approximately ten days after pupation. This will, however, usually vary with each individual. The females do not fly until after they mate and lay eggs (at which time they can be found around ultraviolet light. Males and females will not mate indoors or during the

day. They should be confined in a wire cage in a sheltered place
outdoors. In about two days they will mate, and the female will lay about
200 eggs. Eggs are rarely obtained in captivity in any other way.

The young larvae may be reared together for a while, but the rearing
cage must be cleaned every day or they will die. As soon as the larvae
develop the mature color pattern (black with long white hairs, and a red
"mane") they must be separated, as they are normally solitary creatures.
At this stage overcrowding can bring about drastic losses. However, large
numbers of larvae will still be lost as they mature. For example, perhaps
50 out of an initial 1000 larvae will live to pupate. Nevertheless, these
larvae are quite beautiful and colorful, and well worth the effort.

ISABELLA TIGER MOTH
(Isia isabella)

Background Information

The world-famous woolybear caterpillar can be easily reared all year
long, unlike many other moth species.

Rearing Instructions

These caterpillars feed upon dandelion, dock and plantain, which can
be collected in the fall and potted for winter feeding. In addition the
leaves can be kept in a plastic bag in a refrigerator for several weeks
and still be used for feeding. If the food runs out spinach, lettuce, and
carrot tops can be used as long as they are free of pesticide residues
(wash thoroughly before using).

The larvae go into hibernation during the winter months, and when
rearing this species you can duplicate this by putting the larvae between
the first and second molt into the refrigerator for two to three weeks.
Then return the larvae to room temperature and resume feeding.

Keep actively growing larvae supplied with fresh food, and keep the
cage or rearing container clean at all times. Select a location where the
caterpillars will receive a long day of sunlight, or provide artificial
light for 16 to 18 hours per day. This helps duplicate summertime
conditions.

Yellow woolly bear

TOMATO AND TOBACCO HORNWORMS
(Manduca spp.)

Background Information

Both the tobacco (M. sexta) and tomato hornworm (M. quinquimaculata) may be serious agricultural or garden pests, but they are also easy to rear and provide an great opportunity for studying insect growth and metamorphosis.

Both hornworm species can be reared on tomato plants, so you'll need to grow or buy some spare tomato plants. If you can't find hornworms locally, they can also be purchased from some biological supply houses.

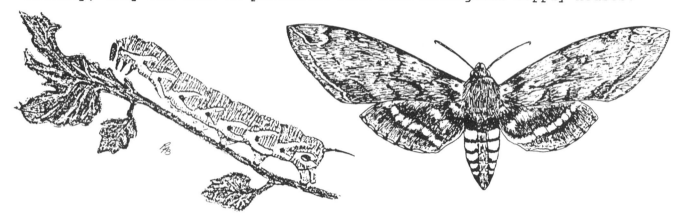

Rearing Instructions

Your caterpillars must be provided with fresh tomato leaves on a daily basis. Large larvae produce lots of frass and it will be necessary to keep the container clean to prevent mold from forming on the frass. When the larvae reach full length, look for signs of pupation (dark horn and black line down the back). Place these larvae in a container filled with shredded paper, sawdust, peatmoss, etc. Wrap a newspaper around the container and place it in a dark place for seven days. Move the container so the pupae are exposed to the daily day and night cycle. Emerging adults may be placed in a large box or cage for mating and egg laying. Place a tomato plant in with the moths and within several days egg laying should begin. These eggs may be used to start another generation of caterpillars.

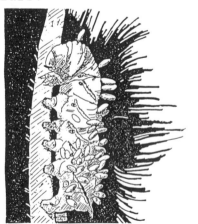

If you collect hornworm caterpillars from the wild, you will occasionally see white cocoons forming on the outside of a caterpillar's body. These are the cocoons of some parasitic wasps (Braconidae) that were feeding inside the caterpillar. Even if the caterpillar successfully forms a pupae it is very unlikely that it will survive to become an adult. Parasitized larvae should be returned to a nearby garden because these parasites are highly beneficial in the control of hornworms.

DEATHSHEAD HAWKMOTH
(Acherontia atropas)

Background Information

The basic requirements essential for successful breeding of this moth are warmth, light, humidity, and larval food plants. As adults, most of the females live for five or six weeks; males for three to four weeks, depending on the conditions in captivity.

Rearing Instructions

Ovae (eggs). Keep the ovae in small plastic boxes and put tissue paper and foodplant leaves in the bottom with 10 ovae per box. All the boxes should have lids. The ovae normally hatch 8 to 10 days after they are laid.

Larvae (caterpillars). After the larvae have hatched and fed on their eggshells, we move them to larger plastic boxes and put slightly damp tissue paper in them. Place 4 to 6 young larvae in each box. The containers should be cleaned and the larvae given fresh food twice a day. When the larvae get to the 3rd and 4th instars they should be moved to larger boxes; in their final stage a half dozen larvae can be moved into a cage. When the larvae leave the food plants to pupate they can be placed in margarine tubs which have damp tissue in them. These tubs should be cleaned daily. The larval stage may be shortened somewhat by raising the temperature.

Larval foodplants include woody nightshade (bittersweet), deadly nightshade, potato, eggplant, privet, and many other plants. If you feed them privet do not attempt to change the larvae to another food plant. Avoid feeding the larvae brown, wilted or sappy leaves; larvae will not eat any food of this description.

Pupae. When the larvae have pupated put then in a large cardboard box with dry tissue paper lining. Small trays are then put in place with pupae on them, about ten to a large box. Check the pupae about once a month. If you want, you can keep them in a breeding cage where they will emerge after a few months. These boxes should be put in a cool, dry place for overwintering. Pad the boxes with cotton wool and do not expose them to temperatures below 55°F. The best ones to overwinter are from late larvae maturing from November to December.

Adult moths. When the pupae turn black they should be taken out of the cardboard boxes and placed into an emergence cage, so that when the moths emerge they have room to dry their wings properly. Do not feed the moths for 2 or 3 days after emergence. After pairing, feed the females every day and the males every other day. The moths are fed honey and water (younger moths get 70% honey and 30% water; older moths get 20% honey and 80% water). Temperatures should be maintained at 68° to 84°F during the day and 68° to 76° at night. A relative humidity of 60 to 70% is best.

WAX MOTH (WAXWORMS)
(Galleria mellonella)

Background Information

The greater wax moth is a pest in honey bee combs, but certain growth characteristics make it suitable for rearing in mass cultures. You can make many valuable observations on the life cycle and biology of insects in your wax moth culture. Also, mature larvae can be harvested and used or sold for fish bait and pet food.

Habits and Life Cycle

Under optimal temperature and humidity conditions, the life cycle (egg hatch to adulthood) of the greater wax moth takes about a month. If conditions are not favorable, development may take much longer. The larvae pass through seven instars. They feed actively in all instars, but grow the most in the final two. The mature larvae spin cocoons and pupae. The adults emerge from these cocoons within a week or two.

Rearing Instructions

Cultures can be started from any stage, but the usual procedure is to collect larvae from infested honey combs or to buy them from a biological supply company. Rear the larvae in a large glass or metal container (they can chew through wood and soft plastic).

Food. In nature the larvae feed on the pollen, honey and beeswax in honey combs. When rearing waxworms in large numbers it is easier to prepare and use a manufactured diet. One such diet, which is inexpensive, easy to use, and that produces favorable results, is made with granular dog food and honey. The food should be prepared as follows. Mix seven parts granular dog food and one part water, then add two parts honey. Mix the ingredients thoroughly and allow them to stand for at least 1 day before using. The dog food granules should be soft, but not sticky.

Habitat. Wax moth cultures will be most successful if you provide them with fairly constant conditions of 90-95° F and 75-85% relative humidity. Add food to the container as it is consumed by the larvae. A continuous cycle of larvae can be obtained by allowing female moths to deposit their eggs on the food in the container. Transfer some adult moths or a few larvae to a fresh container occasionally.

When mature larvae are ready to pupate they will crawl into any available crevice or hollow to spin their cocoons. If you want to "harvest" waxworms, you can take advantage of this behavior by furnishing the culture with a pair of boards with a 1/4-inch gap between them (nails or screws and a few washers can be used to hold the boards apart). Larvae will crawl into this space and can be collected daily. They can be allowed to crawl into rolls of corrugated cardboard strips for holding.

Once the mature larvae have tunneled into the corrugated strips they can be placed in a cool storage area to halt further development. Do not place them in a refrigerator (too cold!). At temperatures near 60° F larvae won't pupate for 2 or 3 months.

ROSY MAPLE MOTH
(Dryocampa rubicunda)

Rearing Instructions

The rosy maple moth is a beautiful moth with sulphur yellow and pastel pink body and wings. The caterpillar stage, known as the green-striped mapleworm, is usually found on red and silver maple. They often feed in colonies, and can sometimes strip a whole tree of leaves.

You can rear these caterpillars by supplying them with fresh maple leaves. Since maple leaves dry out quickly, place the leaves (still attached to the twigs) in water, or use an airtight container to keep the leaves fresh. As the caterpillars get larger, place a piece of paper towel in the bottom of your container to soak up excess moisture. When the larvae are full grown, place peat moss in the bottom of the container. When the caterpillars have successfully formed pupae, move them to a screen cage. After the moths have emerged, watch for mating and egg-laying. If you collect the eggs you can raise another generation of the rosy maple moth.

TENT CATERPILLARS
(Malacosoma spp.)

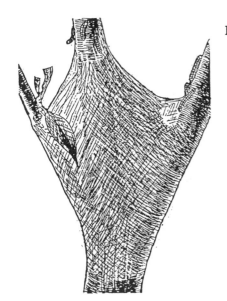

Background Information

Most of us have seen the big silken tents made by these caterpillars, but very few of us have seen the life cycle and developmental stages up close. This common insect is easily raised in the classroom or at home.

Rearing Instructions

Obtain an egg mass from the small branches of wild cherry, apple, plum, or peach trees. This egg mass, found through out late summer, fall, winter and early spring, can be located most easily during the winter when the leaves are off the trees. The eggs masses are about 1/4 inch long and completely encircle the twig, looking something like dried, blackish spittle. Eggs hatch when buds open and new spring leaves start to develop. Bring in some branches of cherry, plum, or apple without egg masses a week or more before the eggs are brought indoors, so there will be a supply of food for the young caterpillars. Supplying an adequate amount of food for the caterpillars if they are started early can be a serious problem. Cut branches placed in water as quickly as possible will remain green if the basal 4 to 5 inches of the branch are cut off under water then placed in a jug or similar container. More than 100 caterpillars may hatch from one egg mass. This number of caterpillars will soon eat all of the small leaves, so be prepared to replenish the food supply as necessary. It will also be necessary to reduced the population to no more than 12-18 caterpillars.

Place the emerging larvae on a sturdy branch (with at least one major "Y-shaped" juncture) bearing fresh foliage. Insert the bottom of the branch into a water bottle and plug up the neck with cotton or paper towel to keep caterpillars from drowning in the water bottle. Setting the branch in a large shallow pan filled with 1-2 inches of water will discourage small caterpillars from wandering away, as long as there is an adequate supply of food. Once a "tent" has been formed the larvae will rest inside, venturing out for food late in the day. The original branch with foliage will be quickly stripped of leaves, so supply fresh food by bringing a second "bouquet" of foliage into contact with the old branch by placing it close enough to the original bottle that some of the branch tips are in contact with one another. Replace with fresh foliage as necessary. The larvae grow quickly and the mature larvae will have a strong urge to leave their home and wander in search of a pupation site, so it is best to transfer them to a cage with soil and twigs at this time. The larvae will spin loose cocoons, and adults should emerge within a week or two.

MEAL MOTHS
(Pyralis farinalis and Plodia interpunctella)

Background Information

Two common types of moths and their larvae that infest stored grains and other foodstuffs in the kitchen can be easily reared. By far the most prevalent of these two is the Indian meal moth.

The adult Indian meal moth is about 3/8 to 1/2 inch (12-14 mm) long. The wings of the adult moth, which are held roof-like over the body, are light grayish-brown on the basal one third and coppery reddish-brown on the outer two thirds. The hind wings are uniformly gray. This distinctive coloration comes from a covering of scales; these scales can and do rub off, making identification a little more difficult at times. The body is tan with reddish-brown head and shoulders. The larvae (caterpillars) are a dirty white or cream color, sometimes tinted with pink or green. When full grown, the larvae measure about 5/8 inch (15 mm).

The female Indian meal moth may lay from 40 to 400 eggs (130 on the average), either singly or in small groups. The eggs are usually deposited directly onto food. The eggs hatch within a few days, and the tiny white caterpillars begin to feed. The caterpillars continue their development over a period of 4 or 5 weeks and then spin a loose, silken cocoon for pupation. The new adult moth will emerge from the cocoon in 10-14 days. The adults only live for a 1 to 2 weeks. Under ideal conditions the entire life cycle can be completed in 6 to 8 weeks, and there can be up to half a dozen generations per year.

The larvae (caterpillars) do all of the feeding. They are general feeders and commonly infest grains and cereals, grain and cereal products, cornmeal (Indian meal), graham flour, dried fruits, nuts, chocolate, cookies and dried pet foods and animal feeds. Less commonly, they may also be found in powdered milk, candies, beans and peas, ground chili pepper, garlic, dried meat, dried mushrooms, garden seeds, and beehive products. If left undisturbed the larvae spin large amounts of silk as they travel and feed. This webbing is often dense enough to attract attention when stored products become heavily infested, and makes the food worthless. Mature larvae usually leave their food when it is time to look for pupation sites. As a result they are often seen climbing up walls and cupboards. The moths are very active during the evening and night-time hours and may be seen flying to indoor lighting, including television screens.

The meal moth may also be found in houses. It is the larger of the two species, having a wingspread of about 1 inch. The body is brownish and the wings are light brown with dark brown patches at both the base and tip, with two distinct, white, wavy lines separating the two shades of brown. The larvae (caterpillars) of this species prefer cereals, cereal and grain products, hay, and many types of dried vegetable matter (especially if the foodstuffs are damp or subject to high humidity). The larvae are also large, about an inch, and they have distinctive black heads.

Rearing Instructions

Any medium to large size glass or plastic container with screen cover is suitable for rearing meal moths. Fill the container with an inch or two of food. The best food can be made from a mixture of whole grain barley, corn, wheat, sunflower seeds, nuts, and/or bird seed (10 parts) plus poultry laying mash (15 parts) and raisins (5 parts). If available, 4 part glycerin should be added as well.

Avoid overcrowding your cultures. When larvae are nearly mature, supply them with pupation sites. Pupation sites can be made by tightly rolling and taping corrugated cardboard into a "log" and then cutting the log into 3/4 inch slices. Periodically transfer some of the occupied pupation sites to new containers with fresh food medium. A separate supply of water is generally not necessary.

MOSQUITOES OR WIGGLERS
(Culicidae)

Larva

Background Information
Everybody knows the mosquito, although not everyone knows that mosquito larvae are aquatic. There are mosquitoes that live in both freshwater and saltwater, including salt marshes, salt lakes, puddles, alpine pools, roadside ditches, woodland pools, tree holes, pitcher plants, freshwater marshes, swamps, ponds, and manmade containers (discarded tires, rain barrels, buckets, etc.).

Mosquito larvae have been nicknamed "wigglers" because of the wiggling motion they make when swimming. These larvae must breathe air and the rear end of their abdomen is equipped with a snorkel-like breathing tube with spiracles at the tip.

Mosquito pupae, on the other hand, are often referred to as "tumblers". Mosquito pupa are quite active, in contrast to most other insect pupae, and can swim about in the water. They must periodically come to the surface of the water to obtain air. The breathing spiracles are located on the thorax of the comma-shaped pupae.

Adults emerge from the pupal skin at the surface of the water, and can alight on the sides of the rearing container or even on the surface of the water. Only females bite (they can be distinguished by the thinner antennae). Males, which feed on pollen and nectar, have bushy antennae.

Rearing Instructions
Mosquito larvae can be collected during the spring and summer months from any of the aquatic sites previously mentioned. Collect them with an old fashioned water dipper, kitchen strainer, or white plastic cup and transport them in a loosely covered container. Also, any uncovered, water-filled container left outdoors will attract egg-laying females.

You can use any watertight container for rearing aquatic insects, but if you use a glass jar or aquarium you'll be able to see the mosquito larvae and pupae. Fishbowls, aquaria, and large, wide-mouth jars all work well. Fill the container half full with unchlorinated water (buy distilled water at the grocery store or use pond water). You can add some aquatic plants if you like (obtained from a pond, stream or pet store). The plants provide food and hiding places, and give off oxygen needed by the insects. You will want to have a screen top for the jar or aquarium, to keep emerging adult mosquitoes from escaping.

Food. Most mosquito larvae are filter feeders, feeding on algae and small bits of organic debris. If you use pond water for rearing it will probably already contain enough food for the larvae. If you use distilled water you will have to supply the larvae with food. Mosquito larvae will eat finely crushed dog biscuits or powdered milk. The tiniest pinch is enough to feed many mosquito larvae.

ANTS
(Formicidae)

Background Information
Ant "farming" has been a fascinating hobby for many generations of nature enthusiasts. Ants are especially interesting because of their social habits. Ants live in colonies where there is a division of labor. The tasks necessary to maintain the colony are divided among three groups (castes) of ants.

Habits and Life Cycle
The workers are responsible for building, maintaining and defending the nest. They also gather food and care for the immatures (ant eggs, larvae and pupae). A single queen lays most of the eggs but she may be assisted by supplemental (auxiliary) reproductive females. At certain times males are also present in the colonies. Because of their complex social system, ants are highly successful insects that inhabit virtually every environment on land.

Rearing Instructions
Ants are easily reared in just about any kind of container, but if you want to observe their activity you will need to use an artificial ant nest or ant farm (also known as a formicarium). Ant farms are available from many biological supply companies and hobby shops, both assembled and in kit form. The typical ant farm is nothing more than two panes of glass or plastic 1 to 3 inches apart and filling with sand or soil.

 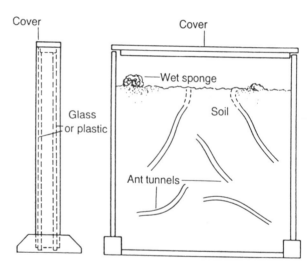

As with many other insects mentioned in this manual, you can either buy your ants or collect your own. Ants can be obtained just about any time of the year, but late July through early September is the best time because you are most likely to find winged, mature ants in or near the nests. All you need to collect ants is a shovel, trowel, kitchen strainer and large (at least gallon-sized) pail or other container with a lid.

The best places to look for ant nests are in fields, vacant lots or any type of open areas. Nests also occur under rocks and trash. Locate an ant hill, preferably a small one in loose, sandy soil. If there is a large mound, remove it with the shovel. Dig into the heart of the nest. Use the trowel and strainer to collect ants and place the ant/soil mixture in your container. Fifty workers should be enough to stock the average artificial ant nest (12 inches by 12 inches). Find and capture the queen

if you can; she'll be bigger than the other ants in the nest. Also
collect samples of any other life stages you see, such as larvae, pupae
("ant eggs" to the non-entomologist) and winged reproductives. You will
also want to take along enough soil to nearly fill the formicarium.
     Fill the ant farm with clean sand or soil. Remove any large clumps of
soil, rocks, vegetation and other debris and place the ant/soil mixture
in the artificial nest. Put the ants and their immature stages on top of
the soil in the formicarium. Cover the glass faces with cardboard and
leave the nest undisturbed for several days. If you don't cover the glass
with an opaque material, the ants are likely to construct their galleries
in the center of the nest and you won't be able to see most of their
activity. Once the colony is established, keep the glass covered when you
aren't observing it, or cover the glass with red acetate to simulate
darkness.
     Food and Water. Most ants are omnivorous and will eat just about
anything. You can feed them dabs of honey thinned with water, molasses
(also thinned), fruit syrup, dead insects, or crumbs and food scraps from
the dinner table. Crackers soaked in sugar water, bread, cake, jam,
jelly, sugar and bits or raw meat are also good foods. Periodically
remove any unused food to prevent mold. Water your ants by placing two
small pieces of wet sponge in the nest. Many nests are built with special
holes in the lid so that you can feed and water the ants without opening
the entire lid.
     The long-term success of your ant farm will depend on whether your
colony has an active queen or supplemental reproductives. If your colony
has no queen it may die out each year, but if you use native species this
is really no problem because you can replace the ants easily.
     Once your ant nest is well-established, you may want to try some other
interesting observations. You can connect your colony to a separate
feeding chamber or to a captive colony of antlions (a predator of ants) by
attaching a length of 3/8-inch to 1/2-inch plastic or rubber tubing
between them. Now you can observe ant foraging behavior or predator/prey
interactions.

TRAP NESTING BEES AND WASPS

Background Information
     While the insect order Hymenoptera is well known for its social
insects (ants, honey bees and yellowjackets), it also includes many
nonsocial or solitary species. These bees and wasps live alone and do not
have the workers, queens, and guards associated with social insects. Many
solitary bees and wasps live in hollow twigs, and in some places are
extremely common.

Biology and Life Cycle
     Most of them have only one generation each year, although a few have
two or three. Bees stock their nests with a pollen/nectar mixture.
Wasps, however, use animal prey and stock their nests with caterpillars,
spiders, aphids, crickets, leafhoppers, and other insects. The females
find the nest, make the cells, and provide food for each cell. She lays
one egg on the food and then makes a cell partition of mud or leaves.
Then she makes more cells until the nest is filled.
     Eggs hatch in 3 or 4 days into small larvae which then feed on the
pollen/nectar or insects. The larvae feed until the food is gone, spins a
cocoon, and rests for the winter. In the spring, the insects will emerge
as an adult bee or wasp.

Rearing Instructions

Since these insects must search for their food, it is difficult to rear them under confined conditions. Another method has been developed which allows for close study and observation of their activity and life cycle. Since some type of hole is required for their nests, trap nests can be made by cutting narrow stripes of wood (6" x 3/4" x 3/4"). Make the strips run along the grain of the wood. Then cut a groove into each strip and mark permanently with a number. Seal one end of each groove with wood filler. Wrap each nest with a sheet of clear plastic or cellophane. Put the cover slip in place to darken the nest. Slip on two rubber bands, one at each end, to hold the nest together. Later you can remove the cover and look inside without harming the inhabitants.

You may want to make a number of these nests and then bundle them together with rubber bands or string. Place bundles of nests in different habitats - in trees, on ledges, window sills, and stairways. Always place them horizontally.

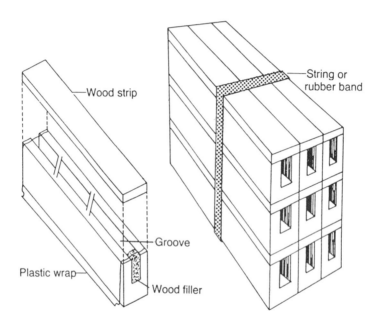

Inspect the traps frequently and keep a notebook with the results of your observations (remember, each nest has its own permanent number). You may want to make notes on the dates of starting and finishing the cells. Check for larvae and parasites.

A quart jar with a cheesecloth lid will serve as an emergence cage. After the larvae spin their cocoons, place them in the emergence cage and wait for the adults to appear.

PART III: NON-INSECT ARTHROPOD REARING

TADPOLE SHRIMP
(Triops spp.)

Background Information

The Eubrachiopoda are members of the order Crustacea that are characterized by a shield-shaped carapace, sessile compound eyes, and 35-71 pairs of leaf-like legs used for swimming and respiration. These creatures are very primitive, dating back 200 million years (Permian) and have not changed (evolved) any since the Triassic. Triops are predators that inhabit temporary bodies of water to are subject to complete drying up during the dry season. These shrimp have evolved a drought-resistant egg stage to cope with these severe environmental conditions. Eggs are also capable of suspending development (diapause) for periods of years. The adults can complete their life cycle in under thirty days, and are capable of hermaphroditic (single parent) reproduction.

Various species of Triops are found worldwide, primarily in tropical regions. Full grown adults reach 1 to 2 inches in length.

Rearing Instructions

Triops eggs in diapause are available for culturing, and demonstrate instant life when the eggs are immersed in water.

Triops are cultured in distilled water (which can be purchased at just about any grocery store). After allowing the water to reach room temperature (73-78°F), with the aid of a lamp if necessary, the eggs are poured into the water. If the water remains at room temperature the eggs should hatch in 18 to 24 hours. Look carefully because the hatching tadpole shrimp are quite tiny and nearly translucent. The growing Triops may be fed small amounts of goldfish or tropical fish food beginning on the fourth day and thereafter they should be fed at least once a day.

Inspect the tank daily to observe the unbelievably rapid growth of Triops, as well as their aquatic "acrobatics" and upside down feeding technique. They quickly mature in under 30 days, and may live for another week or two after reaching maturity. If the water in the tank becomes too cloudy to observe the Triops, gently pour off 1/3 of the water and replace with fresh distilled water. Repeat as necessary. (Pour the water through filter paper and dry the residue for several weeks; later you may be able to start another culture from the eggs in this residue.)

SOWBUGS AND PILLBUGS
(Isopoda)

Background Information

Many species of native sowbugs and pillbugs are easily reared, although their small size is not very exciting. The pillbugs are recognized by their darker color and ability to curl into a tight, circular ball. The sowbugs are similar, but are lighter gray in color and cannot roll into a ball.

Rearing Instructions

Sowbugs and pillbugs are moisture-loving creatures, and are generally kept in plastic boxes, jars, or aquaria with moist (not wet!) peat moss or potting soil in the bottom and a few flat stones and/or large pieces of tree bark. They eat only plant matter, and will feed readily on lettuce, celery, apples, potatoes, and similar fruits and vegetables. They will also eat moist, decaying leaves.

MILLIPEDES
(Diplopoda)

Background Information

Many species of native millipedes are easily reared, although their small size is not very exciting. However, several species of large (greater than 3") tropical millipedes are available through pet shops and make excellent rearing projects.

Rearing Instructions

Millipedes are moisture-loving creatures, and are generally kept in plastic boxes, jars, or aquaria with moist (not wet!) peat moss, crumbled leaf litter, or potting soil in the bottom (and a slab of bark for hiding). They eat only plant matter, and will feed readily on lettuce, celery, apples, grapes, bananas, and similar fruits (not citrus fruits). They also eat moist, decaying leaves. Mist daily with water.

CENTIPEDES
(Chilopoda)

Background Information

Centipedes are basically subterranean, burrowing creatures. They are nocturnal, and the best way to see them is to leave them in a dark room for a few hours and they suddenly turn on the lights. If you are lucky you will probably get a quick glimpse of your centipede before it scurries down the nearest burrow. Centipedes are extremely fast runners and can squeeze through some seemingly impassible cracks.

Centipedes are predators and inject venom through their large chelicerae (poison jaws). The small species, common in the eastern United States, are more or less harmless, perhaps causing a burning sensation at worst. Some of the largest species from the western United States and tropical regions are more likely to cause localized inflammation, pain and temporary paralysis (in adults). Some species have been known to be fatal to small children. (Do not pick up centipedes by hand: use forceps!)

Rearing Instructions

Centipedes are moisture-loving creatures, and are generally kept in tall plastic boxes, jars, or aquaria with moist (not wet!) peat moss, crumbled leaf litter, or potting soil in the bottom (with a slab of bark for hiding). They can be fed small insects (such as mealworms, cricket nymphs, and beetles, or spiders). Mist with water on a daily basis.

DADDY-LONG-LEGS OR HARVESTMEN
(Phalangida)

Rearing Instructions

While most people pick up daddy-long-legs, thinking them totally harmless, but in fact they have very potent venom. However, they are extremely docile and it is difficult to get them to bite, but if you ever get bitten you are in for a nasty surprise. They are not deadly, but may cause extreme pain, inflammation and discoloration of surrounding tissues, and sometimes temporary localized paralysis.

These spider-like arthropods are very docile and easily kept. They can be put in plastic boxes, jars, and aquaria containing peat moss, leaf litter, or potting soil, and like spiders can be fed similar foods. They will also accept bits of bread, beef or mutton fat. Mist occasionally.

GIANT WHIP SCORPION or VINAGAROON
(*Mastigopructus giganteus*)

Rearing Instructions

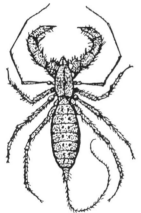

The whip scorpions thrive very easily in captivity, if kept and fed like true scorpions. The giant whip scorpion, also known as the vinagaroon, has a gland at the base of the tail which produces acetic acid which can be sprayed at potential enemies. Acetic acid is a component of vinegar, at a concentration of about 3%. In the glands of the vinagaroon it is found in concentrations of up to 80%! The vinagaroon can spray this acid up to two feet with remarkable accuracy. If the acid gets into the eyes or moist membranes of the attacker, it causes severe irritation, and possibly even blindness. It is therefore advisable to use caution when handling these animals.

SCORPIONS

Background Information

Most people regard all scorpions as deadly and treat them accordingly. There are about 56 species of scorpions in the United States, and only two of these (*Centuroides sculpturaturus* and *C. gertschi*) are poisonous to humans. The stings from most other species are no more severe than a bee sting, but caution is still in order when raising scorpions.

Generally speaking, those species with large pincer claws (pedipalps) are unlikely to be dangerous; those with slender claws usually are dangerous.

Scorpion

For the most part, scorpions are very secretive (many burrow). They are generally active only at night, at which time you may see them walking about or sitting on rocks. Their usual resting stance is with the tail curled up behind and their legs bent and kept close to the body. Their pincers (pedipalps) are extended forward, bent at the first segment. Any disturbance will send them scurrying for cover. While watching scorpions crawling about you will also notice the comb-like pectines between the last pair of legs. These organs are used to test the ground and probably help in prey location.

Rearing Instructions

Plastic boxes or aquaria make an excellent home for most scorpions. Tropical forest species should be provided with humid conditions, a substrate for burrowing (potting soil), and a slab of bark. Desert species can be provided with sand (or dust-free, unscented cat litter) and a few rocks. The container lid can be used to regulate moisture levels: solid with small ventilation holes for humid conditions and screening for dry conditions. Most scorpions require warm temperatures and at times you will find it necessary to keep the cage warm with a suitable pet heater, or an lightbulb (use red whenever possible) suspended over the cage.

One commonly reared species of scorpion is the emperor scorpion (Pandinus imperator) of western Africa. It is large (up to 8"), lives for several years, and is relatively safe (docile and relatively nontoxic). This scorpion prefers humid, tropical conditions and likes to burrow if given suitable medium (potting soil, etc.). Several can be kept together, provided they are about the same size and well-fed. They will eat 1 to 2 crickets per week.

When handling all scorpions use a pair of 10" forceps (tweezers). Grab the scorpion firmly by the tail immediately below the stinger with the forceps. The tail makes a good "handle", being sturdy and having in it some of the strongest muscles in the scorpion, and by holding the tail you can keep the stinger under control.

Basically, scorpions eat the same foods as spiders (small insects and other arthropods). Mealworms (both adults and larvae) and crickets make an ideal source of food for many scorpions. Scorpions should also be provided water in a shallow dish (jar lid, petri dish, or plastic furniture floor guard).

A cage for rearing scorpions

SPIDERS

Biology and Life Cycle

All spiders are predatory, and watching their diverse food gathering and feeding habits is very interesting. There are a few problems with keeping spiders alive. Since they are predatory you must have a supply of living insects to feed them (they will not accept dead insects). For this reason many people who rear spiders, especially tarantulas, also rear fruit flies, crickets, cockroaches, or mealworms as food sources. Spiders are definitely inclined to eat each other, and must be well-fed or kept in separate containers.

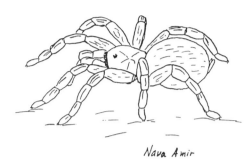

Nava Amir

Sources of Spiders. Like insects, spiders can either be purchased or collected in the wild. Many native North American spiders can be successfully collected and reared. Many people are interested in keeping tarantulas, which are native to many parts of the southwestern United States, Central America, South America, Africa and Asia. While it is possible to collect some tarantulas in the wild, most people buy theirs from a pet shop, livestock dealer, or biological supply company.

Rearing Instructions

Rearing Containers. The type and size of the container is relatively unimportant, as long as it is big enough to let the spider move around freely, and small enough to regulate the humidity if necessary. If your spider is one that normally builds a web to catch its prey, the container must be large enough to hold a web. A gallon jar with several twigs inside to support the web will work well for web-building spiders.

Moisture. An adequate supply of moisture, both in relative humidity and drinking water, is critical for most species of spiders. Placing a piece of wet absorbent cotton in a shallow dish allows spiders easy access to moisture without the risk of drowning. You can also use a cotton-stoppered, water-filled vial; change the cotton every week. The relative humidity of the atmosphere in the container appears to be very important for many spider species. The natural habitat of your spider can serve as a clue to its humidity requirements. Those species which live near water or in the ground require higher relative humidities than other species. Wet the soil in your container so that it remains slightly moist to the touch. Do not over-moisten!

Food. Spiders are predators, which means they require live prey. Lack of or improper food is usually the reason spider raising efforts fail. The feeding problem may be particularly acute with spiderlings (young spiders) that have just emerged from the egg sac. The young of most spider species need food immediately in order to prevent them from eating each other. It is often hard to find prey that is small enough for the young of some species. If you have many spiderlings in a single container you can solve this problem by allowing them to eat each other until some are big enough to accept larger insect food. Another solution is to rear a suitable small insect species, such as flour beetles. The larvae of flour beetles work quite well as spiderling food.

If you plan to rear spiders over the winter months you essentially have no choice but to start a culture of some insect species as a constant food supply. Wingless fruit flies, mealworms, crickets, cockroaches, and caterpillars all work well, especially for larger spiders.

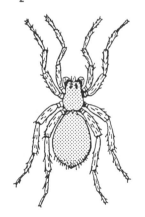

Sanitation. Spiders, like insects, are subject to a variety of diseases. No matter how careful you are, you will still lose some spiders to bacteria and fungi. Healthy spiders have the best chance of avoiding disease, so be sure that your spiders are well-fed and well-watered. Rearing containers should be thoroughly washed and dried between uses. Change the cotton of your water fountain frequently, especially if it has been contaminated by the juices of insects the spider has killed. These juices for a very good medium for the growth of many fungi.

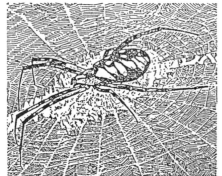

ORB WEAVERS
(Araenidae)

Rearing Instructions

The orb weavers spin intricate webs, and for this reason you may want to build a special cage for these spiders so you can better observe these web building activities. Basically a cage for the orb weavers looks like a large ant farm. Take two large pieces of glass or plexiglass about two to three feet square and make a wooden frame to hold the plates about three inches apart. Inside such a cage the spider will build a beautiful web almost filling the box, using the four attachment points as it would use branches or weed stems in the wild. Food can be dropped into the web through holes drilled in the top and plugged with corks.

As an alternative to this, it is also possible to build an open-air "stage" for orb weavers. Obtain a board about 18 to 24 inches long and drill two holes near each end. Dowels or tree branches are inserted upright into these holes and serve as attachment points for the orb web. Placing the board in a large "moat" of water will prevent the spider from wandering away.

TARANTULAS

Background Information

Contrary to popular belief, most tarantulas are not dangerous, although they will bite if handled roughly. The bites are painful (like a bee sting) but not fatal. Much of the localized pain and swelling is a result of germs transmitted during the bite. Tarantulas have urticating hairs on their abdomens, and if these come in contact with the skin they may cause skin rashes (which usually disappear in a day or two).

Although some tarantulas are easily handled, the risk of hurting the spider is great, so handle your spider only when absolutely necessary. The best way to move a spider is with a rectangular fish net. Gently prod

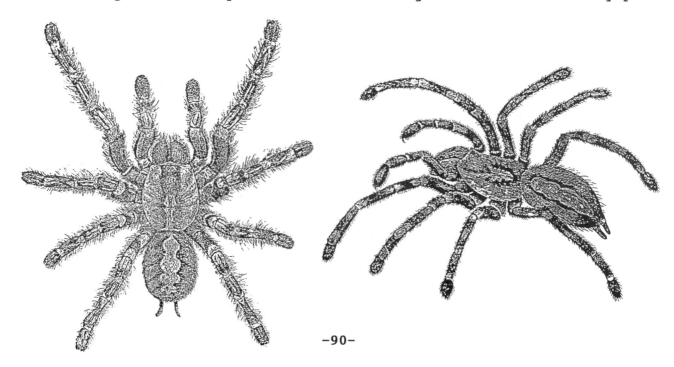

the spider into it moves into the net, then seal the opening with a piece of cardboard. This method works well for nasty spiders and escapees!

Biology and Life Cycle

Whereas most spiders only live for a year or so, female tarantulas may survive for up to 20 years. When you buy a tarantula, try to get a female or an immature male, because mature males will only live for another year or so! Look at the "knee joint" of the first pair of legs. If the joint has small pair of thumb-like projections, then the spider is a mature male. Don't buy that one if you want a long-term pet.

Tarantulas build large irregular webs on the ground, often covering an area of up to 12 square inches. Sitting at the edge of the web with their pedipalps on the web, they wait until some small prey such as an insect or lizard walks over it. The tarantula feels the vibration through the web and pounces on the prey and then has dinner. They may also apply thin (invisible!) webbing to the sides of aquaria which enables them to climb the sides of the container with ease. Tarantulas are great escape artists, and a secure lid is a must!

Rearing Instructions

Tarantulas require nearly the same conditions as other spiders. A terrarium with sand, soil, or peat moss in the bottom makes an ideal container, depending on the moisture requirements of the species. Many breeders like to use vermiculite because it is inorganic, sterile and lightweight. It is not good to keep the sand or vermiculite moist in the case of those species that inhabit deserts or other dry habitats, as they may get a fungus infection on their feet and consequently lose their feet or die. Many species like to burrow (if given sufficient substrate), but you can make a nice "artificial" burrow out of a piece of florists foam. Cut a circular, slanting tunnel through the top of the foam. On the underside of the foam gouge out a large chamber. If you make this chamber offset to one side you will be able to see the tarantula in its burrow when the foam is in place. Place the foam in one corner of an empty terrarium and fill the remainder of terrarium bottom with vermiculite.

As a general rule, never place more than one tarantula in a terrarium, because they are strongly cannibalistic! Of course, if you are trying to breed tarantulas you will have to put a male and female together for a period of time. Make sure they are both well fed before putting them together. This will reduce the chances of one spider killing the other.

Tarantulas require both food and water. Hungry tarantulas will try to eat just about anything that moves and is smaller than they are (spiders, large insects, small snakes, lizards, toads and baby mice). They can also be tricked into eating canned dog food or ground beef. Do this by forming a small ball of meat around the end of a piece of thread and then jiggling it in front of the spider. When the spider grabs the bait, keep jiggling the string while you gently pull the string out of the meat. The spider will think the "prey" is struggling to get away and should then really hold on to it.

One large insect a week is enough for most tarantulas. During spring, summer and fall most tarantula species should be fed every 4 or 5 days. During winter the spiders seldom eat, but it's a good idea to offer them food once every other week. It is impossible to overfeed tarantulas; they will only eat according to their needs. Water can be provided by placing moist cotton in a shallow dish and putting it in the spider's terrarium.

If you should happen to find your tarantula on its back don't be concerned, and DON'T disturb the spider. The spider molts in this position and turning it over will interfere with the molting process. Slightly higher humidity is also important at this time.

RESOURCES
Bibliography of Insect and Arthropod Rearing Information

The following partial bibliography gives you a list of books and journal articles that provide helpful information on rearing insects. The staff at your local library or at the Young Entomologists' Society will probably be able to help you locate these publications.

Alderton, David. 1992. A Step by Step Book About Stick Insects. T.F.H. Publications, Neptune City, NJ 64pp.

Alya, A.B. and F.P. Hain. 1987 Rearing Monochamus species larvae on artificial diet (Coleoptera: Cerambycidae). J. Econ. Entomol. 80:427-432

Anonymous. 1970. Rearing the Greater Wax Moth. USDA Science Study Aid No. 3, 6pp.

Anonymous. 1982. Carolina Arthropods Manual. Carolina Biological Supply Co., Burlington, NC.

Banks, W.A. et al. 1981. Techniques for Collecting, Rearing, and Handling Imported Fire Ants. USDA, SEA, Advances in Agr. Technol. Bull A 106.24:S-21, 9pp.

Bardwell, J. and S. Prchal. 1988. Bug Ranching: A Primer for Livestock Husbandry. Backyard Bugwatching No. 5, pp. 9-16

Blasi, K. and N.L. Wallace. 1984. Raising Grasshoppers. Carolina Tips 47(6)

Bornancin, B. 1985. Small Animals in Captivity. Burke Books, London and New York. 31pp.

Brewer, J. and D. Winter. 1986. Butterflies and Moths - A Companion to Your Field Guide. Prentice-Hall, Englewood Cliffs, NJ. 194pp.

Brock, Paul D. 1985. Phasmid Rearer's Handbook (Stick and Leaf Insects). Publication #20, Amateur Entomologists Society, Hanwell, UK

Brown, Vinson. 1987. How to Make a Miniature Zoo. Dodd, Mead and Co., New York, NY.

Brown, Vinson. 1983. Investigating Nature Through Outdoor Projects. Stackpole Books, Harrisburg, PA.

Buck, Margaret W. 1958. Pets from the Pond. Abingdon Press, New York. 244pp.

Busvine, J.R. 1955. Simple Methods for Rearing the Cricket (Gryllus domesticus L.) With Some Observations on the Speed of Development at Different Temperatures. Proc. Royal Entomol. Soc. London 30:15-18.

Cate, J.R. 1987. A method of rearing parasitoids of boll weevil without the host plant. Southwest Entomol. 12:211-215

Conklin, Gladys. 1966. The Bug Club Book. A Handbook for Young Bug Collectors. Holiday House, Garden City, NY.

Conklin, Gladys. 1978. Praying Mantis - The Garden Dinosaur. Holiday House, New York, NY. 30pp.

Corriher, Charles M. 1985. Modern Drosophila Care. Carolina Tips 48(2)

Cummins, K. W. et al. 1984. Experimental Entomology. Reinholt Publ. Co., New York. 176pp.

Dahm, P.A. 1955. A Convenient Method For Rearing Large Cockroaches. Journal of Economic Entomology 48(4):480-482.

Danks, Hugh V. 1987. The Bug Book. Workman Publishing, New York, NY.

David, Al. 1987. Tarantulas: A Complete Introduction. TFH Publications, Neptune City, NJ.

de Vosjoli, Philippe. 1991. Arachnomania. The General Care and Maintenance of Tarantulas and Scorpions. Advanced Vivarium Systems. Lakeside, CA. 79pp.

Dickerson, W.A. et al. 1979. Arthropod Species in Culture in the United States and Other Countries. Entomol. Society of America, Lanham, MD.

Dowd, P.F. 1987. A labor-saving method for rearing the dried fruit beetle (Coleoptera: Nitidulidae) on pinto bean diet. J. Econ. Entomol. 80:1351-1353

Dunn, Gary A. 1988. Insect Life Cycle Studies. Cooperative Extension Service, Michigan State University, East Lansing, MI

Dunn, G.A. 1992. The Insect Study Sourcebook (4th Ed.). Special Publication No. 1, Young Entomologists' Society, 1915 Peggy Place, Lansing MI 48910, 91pp.

Dutky, et al. 1962. A Technique for Mass Rearing the Greater Wax Moth (Lepidoptera: Galleriidae). Proc. Entomol. Soc. Wash. 64(1):56-58.

Ewbank, Constance. 1973. Insect Zoo. How to Collect and Care for Insects. Walker and Co., New York. 96pp.

Floyd, Dorothy. 1991. Keeping Stick Insects. Floyd Publishing, Bottesford, UK. 60pp.

Ford, R.L.E. 1973. Studying Insects. A Practical Guide. Frederick Warne and Co., New York. 150pp.

Friedrich, Ekkehard. 1983. Breeding Butterflies and Moths. A Practical Handbook for British and European Species. Harley Books, Colchester, UK. 173pp.

Galford, Jimmy R. 1969. Artificial Rearing of 10 Species of Wood-boring Insects. USDA Forest Service Research Note NE-102, pp. 1-6

Gangwere, S.K. 1960. The Feeding and Culturing of Orthoptera in the Laboratory. Entomol. News 71(1/2):7-45

Gardiner, B.O.C. 1987. Rearing the painted lady Cynthia cardui L. with particular reference to the use of semi-synthetic diet. Entomol. Rec. 99: 205-214

Ghouri, A.S.K. and J.E. McFarlane. 1958. Observations on the Development of Crickets. Canadian Entomol. 90:158-165.

Harley, K.I.S. and B.W. Willson. 1968. Propogation of a Cerambycid Borer on a Meridic Diet. Canad. J. Zool. 46:1265-1266

Haydak, M.H. 1936. A Food for Rearing Laboratory Insects. Journal of Economic Entomology 29(5):1026.

Hawes, Judy. 1972. My Daddy-long-legs. Thomas Crowell Co., New York. 34pp.

Headstrom, Richard. 1982. Adventures With Insects. Dover Publications, New York, NY.

Heal, Ralph E. 1948. Rearing methods for German and American cockroaches. J. Econ. Entomol. 41:329-330

Heath, G.L. 1980. Rearing and Studying the Praying Mantids. Leaflet #36, Amateur Entomol. Society, Hanwell, UK.

Henwood, Chris. 1988. Keeping Minibeasts. Spiders. Franklin Watts, Inc., London, UK.

Hogner, Dorothy Childs. 1951. Odd Pets. Scholastic Inc., New York. 128pp.

Hogner, Dorothy Childs. 1963. Water Beetles. Thomas Crowell Co., New York, NY.

Hopf, Alice. 1965. Monarch Butterflies. Thomas Crowell and Co., New York. 134pp.

Hull-Williams, Vince. 1986. How to Keep Scorpions. Fitzgerald Publishing, London, UK.

Hussey, L. and C. Pessino. 1953. Collecting Cocoons. Thomas Crowell Co., New York, NY. 73pp.

Hussey, L. and C. Pessino. 1975. Collecting for the City Naturalist. Thomas Crowell Co., New York, NY. 72pp.

Jansen, D.H. 1988. The Foodplants of Costa Rican Saturniids and Sphingids. Amateur Entomol. Soc. Bull. 47:108-113

Kelly, H.A. 1903. Silkworm Culture. USDA Farmer's Bull. No. 105. 32pp.

Kramer, David C. 1989. Animals in the Classroom. Addison-Wesley, Reading, MA. 234pp.

Krull, Wendell H. 1929. The rearing of dragonflies from eggs. Annals Entomol. Soc. Amer. 22:651-658

Lamb, R.Y. and R.B. Wiley. 1987. Maintaining cave crickets (Orthoptera: Rhaphlodophoridae). Entomol. News 98:147-149

Lanciani, C.A. 1987. Rearing immature Mesovelia mulsanti (Hemiptera: Mesoveliidae) on a substratum of duckweed. Florida Entomol. 70:286-288

Lippold, P.C. 1967. Processing of Milkweed Seeds and Notes on Laboratory Rearing of the Large Milkweed Bug. Journal of Economic Entomol. 60(2):491-493.

Lund, Dale. 1977. All About Tarantulas. T.F.H. Publications, Neptune City, NJ.

Mayer, D.F. and C.C. Mayer. 1979. How to Rear Insects for Fun and Profit. Bug-Gone-It Press, Yakima, WA.

Meyers, Susan. 1991. Insect Zoo. Lodestar Books, New York. 48pp.

Mitchell, Arthur A. 1964. First Aid for Insects and Much More. Harvey House, Inc., Irvington-On-Hudson, NY.

Morgan, Randy. 1988. Windows on the Water World. Backyard Bugwatching No. 5, pp. 4-8

Murphy, Frances. 1980. Keeping Spiders, Insects and Other Land Invertebrates in Captivity. J. Bartholomew and Son, Ltd., Edinburgh, UK.

Norsgaard, E. Jaedecker. 1988. How to Raise Butterflies. Dodd, Mead and Co., New York, NY.

Oda, H. 1986. Insects in the Pond. Raintree Publishers, Milwaukee. 32pp.

O'Hagen, Caroline. 1980. It's Easy to Have a Caterpillar Visit You. Lothrup, Lee and Shephard, New York. 22pp.

Ottens, R.J. and G.A. Herzog. 1987. A greenhouse rearing technique for larvae of the whitefringed beetle, Graphognathus peregrinus (Buchanan) (Coleoptera: Curculidae). J. Entomol. Sci. 22:352

O'Toole, Christopher. 1986. Discovering Ants. Bookwrights Press, New York. 46pp.

Perrero, Laurie and Lewis. 1979. Tarantulas in Nature and as Pets. Windward Publishing, Inc., Miami, FL.

Peterson, Alvah. 1934. A Manual of Entomological Equipment and Methods. Edwards Bros., Ann Arbor, MI.

---- 1964. Entomological Techniques. Columbus, OH.

Pohl, Kathleen. 1987. Hermit Crabs. Raintree Publishers, Milwaukee. 32pp.

Pohl, Kathleen. 1987. Crayfish. Raintree Publishers, Milwaukee. 32pp.

Pronek, Neal. 1982. Land Hermit Crabs. TFH Publications, Neptune City, NJ.

Pyle, Robert M. 1992. Handbook for Butterfly Watchers. Houghton-Mifflin, Boston. 274pp.

Roberts, Hortense Roberta. 1974. You Can Make an Insect Zoo. Charles Scribner's Sons, New York, NY.

Roberts, Mervin F. 1978. All About Land Hermit Crabs. T.F.H. Publications, Neptune City, NJ.

Selander, Richard. 1986. Rearing Blister Beetles (Coleoptera: Meloidae). Insecta Mundi 1(4):209-220

Severin, H.H.P. and H.C. Severin. 1911. A Few Suggestions on the Care of the Eggs and Rearing of the Walkingstick, Diapheromera femorata Say. Psyche 18(4):121-123

Simon, Seymour. 1987. Pets in a Jar. Collecting and Caring for Small Wild Animals. Viking Press, New York, NY.

Singh, Pritam. 1977. Artificial Diets for Insects, Mites and Spiders. Plenum Press, New York, NY.

Singh, Pritam and R.F. Moore. 1985. Handbook of Insect Rearing (Vols. 1 and 2). Elsevier Science Publishers, New York, NY.

Singh, Pritam. 1986. Insect Rearing. New Zealand DSIR Extension Information, Bulletin #53, March 1986.

Siverly, R.E. 1962. Rearing Insects in Schools. W.C. Brown Co., Dubuque, IA.

Smith, Robert W. 1987. Critters in the Classroom. Instructional Fair, Grand Rapids, MI.

Smithers, Courtney. 1981. Handbook of Insect Collecting. AH & AW Reed, Sydney, Australia. 120pp.

Solomon, J.D. 1966. Artificial Breeding of the Carpenterworm, _Prionoxystus robiniae_ (Lepidoptera: Cossidae), and Observations of its Development. Annals Entomol. Soc. Amer. 59:1197-1200

Spooner, Sally. 1987. How to Raise the Monarch Butterfly. Spooner Press, Lakeville, MA.

Sterling, Dorothy. 1961. Caterpillars. Doubleday and Co., Garden City, NY.

Stevens, Carla. 1961. To Catch a Cricket. Addison-Wesley, Reading, MA.

Stevens, Carla. 1978. Insect Pets: Catching and Caring for Them. Greenwillow/Morrow, New York, NY.

Stokes, D. & L. and E. Williams. 1991. The Butterfly Book. Little, Brown and Co., Boston.

Stone, J.L.S. 1992. Keeping and Breeding Butterflies and Other Exotica. Blanford Publishing, London. 192pp.

Stone, J.L.S. and H.J. Midwinter. 1975. Butterfly Culture: A Guide to Rearing Butterflies, Moths and Other Insects. Blanford Press, Dorset, UK.

Strong, R.G. et al. 1968. Rearing Stored Product Insects for Laboratory Studies: Six Species of Moths. J. Econ. Entomol. 61:1237-1249

Tekulsky, Matthew. 1985. The Butterfly Garden. Turning Your Garden, Window Box or Backyard Into a Beautiful Home for Butterflies. Harvard Common Press, Cambridge, MA.

Villiard, Paul. 1973. Insects as Pets. Doubleday and Co., NY. 143pp.

Villiard, Paul. 1975. Moths and How to Rear Them. Funk and Wagnalls, New York, NY.

Watts, Barrie. 1990. Keeping Minibeasts: Ants. Franklin Watts, New York. 29pp.

Watts, Barrie. 1989. Keeping Minibeasts: Beetles. Franklin Watts, New York. 29pp.

Watts, Barrie. 1991. Keeping Minibeasts: Butterflies and Moths. Franklin Watts, New York. 29pp.

Watts, Barrie. 1991. Keeping Minibeasts: Grasshoppers and Crickets. Franklin Watts, New York. 29pp.

Watts, Barrie. 1990. Keeping Minibeasts: Ladybugs. Franklin Watts, New York. 29pp.

Watts, Barrie. 1991. Keeping Minibeasts: Woodlice and Millipedes. Franklin Watts, New York. 29pp.

Watts, Barrie. 1991. Keeping Minibeasts: Stick Insects. Franklin Watts, New York. 29pp.

Webb, Ann. 1992. The Proper Care of Tarantulas. TFH Publications. Neptune City, NJ. 288pp.

Wilcox, J.A. 1972. Entomology Projects for Elementary and Secondary Schools. Bulletin 422, New York State Museum and Science Service, Albany, NY.

Wineriter, S.A. and T.J. Walker. 1988. Group and Individual Rearing of Field Crickets (Orthoptera: Gryllidae). Entomol. News 99(1):53-62

Wollerman, E.H. et al. 1969. Continuous Laboratory Culture of the Locust Borer, _Megacyllene robiniae_. Annals Entomol. Soc. Amer. 62(3):647-649

APPENDIX A
Commercial Sources for Artificial Diets
BioServe, Inc. (P.O. Box 450, Frenchtown, NJ 08825)
Connecticut Valley Biol. Supply Co. (P.O. Box 326, Southampton, MA 01073)
Southern Biological Supply Co. (P.O. Box 68, McKenzie, TN 38201)
Stonefly Industries (P.O. Box 4264, Bryan, TX 77805-4264)
Ward's Natural Science Establishment (P.O. Box 92912, Rochester, NY 14623)

APPENDIX B
Y.E.S. Policy on the Collection of Insects
The collection of insect specimens is recognized as an appropriate, valid and necessary activity, well founded in scientific procedure and investigation. Furthermore, this Society recognizes that important contributions can be made to entomological science through the collection of insect specimens by recreational and amateur collectors, as long as such activity is ecologically sound and within the constraints of appropriate guidelines. In so much as insects are a renewable natural resource, this Society recognizes the right of members to collect specimens for display and study, providing the following guidelines and practices which assure preservation and maintenance of biological diversity in perpetuity are met.

We join with other concerned entomological societies and organizations in urging our members to adhere to these, or similar, guidelines.

PURPOSES OF COLLECTING: (1) create reference collections for study and appreciation; (2) document regional diversity, frequency, variability of species as well as representation in environments undergoing or threatened with alteration by man or natural forces; (3) serve as voucher specimens for published records and checklists; (4) compliment a planned research endeavor; (5) aid in dissemination of educational information; and (6) augment our understanding of taxonomic and ecological relationships.

RESTRAINTS ON NUMBERS OF SPECIMENS. Collection of insects should be limited to sampling, not depleting, populations. When collecting where the size of the population is unknown, caution and restraint should be exercised until extent and/or fragility is determined. The use of reared material for obtaining specimens is encouraged. Field collecting should be selective, when possible. When trapping is employed, live traps are preferred to killing traps (which should only be used for planned studies). In any event, all traps should be checked on a regular basis so as to prevent needless destruction of insects.

ENVIRONMENTAL AND LEGAL CONSIDERATIONS. Collection of insect specimens must be undertaken in such a manner as to minimize damage to the environment (habitat, foodplants, etc.). Collectors are also obligated to comply with all laws and regulations concerning collection on public lands, protection of rare, threatened or endangered species or habitats, and transportation and importation of live material.

STEWARDSHIP OF COLLECTED MATERIAL. Collectors are responsible for the following: (1) preservation of specimens with complete data attached; (2) protection of specimens from light, mold, pests and physical damage; (3) collections should be made available for examination by qualified researchers; (4) type specimens (especially holotypes and allotypes) should be deposited in an appropriate institutional collection; (5) specimens or collections, plus any associated written or photographic records, should be offered or willed to an appropriate scientific institution if the collector losses interest, or lacks space, or in anticipation of death. The Young Entomologists' Society stands ready to assist in locating an appropriate depository for specimens or collections.